just keep breathing

UNFILTERED thoughts ON life AFTER LOSS, the struggle of grief, AND learning TO hope again

JORDAN TATE

WESTBOW
PRESS®
A DIVISION OF THOMAS NELSON
& ZONDERVAN

WestBow Press books may be ordered through booksellers or by contacting:

WestBow Press
A Division of Thomas Nelson & Zondervan
1663 Liberty Drive
Bloomington, IN 47403
www.westbowpress.com
1 (866) 928-1240

ISBN: 978-1-5127-9678-0 (sc)
ISBN: 978-1-5127-9679-7 (e)

Library of Congress Control Number: 2017911475

Print information available on the last page.

WestBow Press rev. date: 11/07/2017

Acknowledgements

For Ellie and Elsie.
Chris, thank you for asking me to marry you.
You are the greatest man I have ever met.
My family, thank you for being the most
nurturing family on the planet.
Sarah and Megan, this book would
not exist without the two of you and
your unwavering friendship.

1

The Beginning

I suppose this journey of ours began long before my husband and I knew each other, but meeting each other is probably a good place to start. I decided to transfer schools after my freshman year of college because, naturally, I picked the wrong one first. I mean, I guess there isn't really a "wrong school," but rather I chose a school that did not jibe well with my personality or interests. When I told my parents I wanted to switch, they said, "We figured that would happen."

Their response accurately conveys who I am at the very core of my being. I am independent to a fault—and too stubborn to admit it. I certainly do not pride myself on my ability to do most things the hard way first, but I consistently find myself diving headfirst into situations that I know, deep down, are not ideal. Transferring schools was not one of those situations.

It was one of the first decisions I made in my life that felt really right. The transition to the school that better fit my career goals and personality was surprisingly smooth—besides the fact that I opened my housing assignment letter to find that I did not get my first, second, or even third choice of university housing. I was assigned to an on-campus apartment complex that was close to last on my list. It's funny to stand where I am now and look back on all of the situations that I perceived to be problematic at the time. I am positive I cried over this. Needless to say, I tried to remain cautiously optimistic as I packed my then-current dorm room into boxes and headed off to a brand-new town.

My parents drove me up to my new college home on move-in day, and I was pleasantly surprised—thanks to my previously terrible attitude—that I really liked the inside of the apartment to which I was assigned. It turned out that the apartment last on my list wasn't so shabby after all. It was spacious and had a full kitchen, and I settled in quickly.

This new town was a far cry from the one I left in the middle of a busy city. It was refreshing and quiet, and it was fitted with open fields and trees all around; there was an almost tangible, adventurous spirit in the air. Later on in the day during my move, I was able to meet most of my neighbors, all of whom seemed incredibly friendly. It wasn't long before I had established some strong friendships with the guys in the apartment next door to me. A couple of friends of mine, and the guys in that apartment, ended up becoming really close as we shared meals and adventures together during our free time from studying.

I remember always being able to tell when they were home because the wall that we shared, along with the floor, would shake loudly as they played video games in between studying. As one would expect from four college boys. The shaking was probably from the speakers they had set up. Or the jumping. I could also tell when one roommate in particular was home because I would hear the not-so-subtle beat of the conga drums that he played in between classes. His name was Chris.

It honestly was a good year of bonding and fellowship—and, naturally, very little sleep. In fact, it was such a good year that we all signed up to be neighbors again the following year in an on-campus apartment complex close by.

Although I did casually date a couple of people that first year, I left for my job as a summer camp counselor slightly discouraged in the realm of dating and relationships. I had been hurt quite a few times. Mostly, I was unsure if I was even interested in having another serious relationship until later in life. The camp I worked at was an all-girls camp, so I had plenty of months to pray and think about it without the presence of boys around. I'm convinced this was the most clarifying, refreshing situation that could have happened that summer.

One day, while I was having some alone time, I was prompted to journal and pray about the qualities in a future spouse that I desired—whether serious or trivial—and then pray about them and surrender them to God. This was one of the first times I was able to admit that I needed some divine intervention (independent to a fault, remember?), and I assume God said "Finally." It ended up being a really fruitful time of prayer that I walked away from feeling liberated. I finished up my summer in the mountains of North Carolina and excitedly prepared to head back to school and catch up with friends.

Upon returning to school that next fall, my roommates and I moved in alongside our close friends from the year before, and we all settled into the chaos of classes, extracurriculars, and studying. I got really close with one of the guys in particular, because we both had experienced difficult relationships the previous year that we hadn't fully processed, even after our summers of growth. This is not to mention that his other three roommates were all in long-distance relationships, and were out of town almost every weekend. We talked about what we had been through, what we wish we could have changed about the previous year, and how we felt God was working. I told him that I had given up my desire to date anyone seriously, and that I was glad to have my focus elsewhere. His thoughts were the same, and we were happy that we could help one another realize that dating is for suckers and that it was going to be a good year of zero heartbreaks and no relationship drama. Victory.

Naturally, it wasn't long after that the two of us discovered we were dealing with some strong feelings for one another that made no sense at all considering we had never viewed each other as anything but platonic friends. *I'm sorry. Did we not just discuss how liberated we were in our singleness?* Sounds random and sudden, right? That's what we said. Trust me when I say that no part of the story is missing here. At the time I thought I was the only one working through these startling feelings for my "friend," but it turns out he was dealing with the same thing on his end—and his feelings for me began right around the same time as mine did for him. This definitely wasn't part of the plan; I had to remain single throughout this next year. The situation was absolutely as out-of-the-blue as it seems. We found ourselves flirting and spending most of our free time together, all the while wondering if the other one was feeling the same way. After weeks of this madness had gone by, we ended up having a surprisingly comfortable talk about our sudden attraction to one another. We went from being purely platonic friends to desiring an exclusive, committed relationship in mere weeks.

I'll never forget the day I called my mom to tell her that Chris and I were a potential "thing." It was before we had officially decided to start dating, and I said something like, "Mom … I'm pretty sure there's something going on between Chris and me."

She replied, "Your neighbor Chris?"

I remember talking to her about one particularly stressful time a couple weeks prior where I had developed a horrible migraine. I had never had a migraine before, so I wasn't sure how to handle it. I didn't even feel well enough to drive to a store to get medication for it. I later found out that the migraine occurred because of a medication I was on, but all of my roommates were gone. I had never experienced head pain like that. I was by myself in my apartment, unsure of how to handle it.

For reasons I understand now, Chris was the first person I thought of to reach out to, even though I had not yet acknowledged (or even recognized) any romantic feelings toward him. I texted him to tell him I was feeling really awful, and he came over almost immediately and rummaged around my freezer for a bag of frozen food to hold to my forehead as I lay on my couch—looking as unattractive as ever and not caring at all.

About a month later, our friendship had progressed to the point that we were spending most of our weekend nights watching movies or talking in my apartment until the wee hours of the morning. We had begun to sit particularly close to one another—close enough to distract me during our movie nights as I pondered if he was just being flirtatious, or if he had developed feelings for me.

One night after a movie ended, I could no longer handle all the questions spinning around in my head, so I worked up the courage to ask him what the deal was with our undefined relationship. In case you're wondering, this is still how I like to do business. Straight and to-the-point. I may have felt bold in my inquiry, but I perspired more than I would like to admit while waiting for his response. I was almost sure he was going to tell me he was sorry for leading me to believe there was more going on than purely friendship. Luckily for me, he told me that he definitely liked me as "more than a friend," and after having a pretty deep conversation about romantic relationships and expectations, he asked me to be his girlfriend.

The start of our relationship was a far cry from the ones I had experienced in the past. It just felt so different and refreshing and genuine. I think it helped that we had already known each other so well from being neighbors the previous year. We had each gotten to know one another while in other relationships, so we were never trying to impress each other or only reveal what we thought were our best sides. We saw each other day-in and day-out, and it wasn't easy to hide.

To this day, Chris teases me about what happened after he asked me to be his girlfriend, as it may very well be my most embarrassing moment in our history together. I was more excited than I had ever been before about being someone's girlfriend. I was no longer fumbling around in the weird world of a blurry, undefined relationship and I had nothing but good feelings and no reservations about the fact that we were now dating.

Chris thought that making our relationship official was reason enough to attempt to kiss me for the first time, and I wish I could tell you it was magical and mind-blowing except I can't, because I couldn't stop smiling. No, seriously. I couldn't stop smiling to the point that Chris kept trying to give me kisses that landed solely on my teeth, and then he would laugh and I would laugh (to keep from crying) and he would try again. (Yes, it was humiliating, thanks for asking.) After several more attempts, he quit trying and settled on a hug, and then he walked the long, twenty-five foot walk back to his apartment next door.

I spent the next three hours debating whether or

not he was going to change his mind about me before the morning due to the fact that our first kiss ended horribly and I had probably caused his attraction towards me to disappear instantly. There's a lot riding on that first kiss, said every romantic movie I had ever watched. I am happy to report that he didn't change his mind about me, but he takes much enjoyment from reminding me of how awkward and hilarious smile-kisses are. That being said, I purposely teeth-kiss him now just to reminisce on the good ole' days.

The day after our awkward first kiss, we went on a date to the tennis court on campus. I stressed out the entire way there, thinking that he was taking me on a super un-romantic date so that he could break up with me afterwards by explaining that we are much better off remaining friends (because of the teeth kiss.) My fears were amplified by the fact that I totally left my hand available at my side for him to hold, but he never grabbed it. (I no longer recommend this as a way to determine if your partner is into you or not.)

I nervously played tennis and waited for him to let me down softly, but he never did. I even tried really hard to beat him at tennis so he might change his mind about our awful kiss and keep me. I did beat him, by the way. I know you were wondering.

The good news is our tennis game ended and we walked all the way home without him breaking up with me. He even tried to kiss me again later so

I knew we were still going strong in our one-day-old relationship. This time I forced myself to hold back the smiles and offer an actual kiss, as opposed to a teeth kiss, in return. I told him months later about my hand-holding-first-date theory and subsequent belief of our impending relationship doom, and he laughed hysterically at the ways in which my brain works. He never again let my hand sway lonely at his side.

I was most nervous when it came time to introduce Chris to my family. They had met Chris in passing when they visited me, but they had only ever met him as a "neighbor-friend" of mine. He ended up fitting in well when he met everybody, but he was still a bit shy around them for the first couple of months of our relationship. He eventually came to my parent's house with me around Christmas time, after we had been dating for about three months. My parents thought it would be a good weekend to go Christmas tree shopping; my most favorite holiday tradition! When we returned home with the Christmas tree, Chris took it upon himself to work on stringing the lights around it. Chris had not yet opened up completely around my family, as is normal anytime you meet new people. But I knew they had yet to meet his silly side--a side of his personality that I really admire.

Chris worked his way behind the Christmas tree in the corner of the room and, once out of sight by all, instinctively began singing a Christmas carol quite loudly in a funny, exaggerated voice. I didn't think anything special about what was happening, as I saw this side of him frequently, but all of my family members there completely lost it. They were finally introduced to the Chris that I knew so well. The best part about the whole situation was that he simply forgot they were around. From then on, Chris got more and more comfortable around my family, and they began to see him as I did: silly, light-hearted, caring, intelligent, and strong, always putting my needs far before his own.

We spent the next several months cooking together, running around campus, and hammocking amongst all of the lovely trees on our campus. We talked of marriage frequently, as it didn't take us long to realize we never wanted to do life without one another. We enjoyed sharing conversation about our future dreams, goals, and desires, including one of which was to make a lot of babies.

Nine months after our awkward first kiss we were engaged, and nine months after that we were husband and wife. About halfway through our dating months, I remembered the conversation I had had with God while away at summer camp, and I scrambled to find my journal to read what I had written. Turns out that, when writing about what I thought my future spouse would be like, I had described Chris' personality to a T, as well as his hobbies and physical appearance--down to his exact eye color, never once realizing I was describing someone that I already knew.

I know what you're thinking, I must have known, deep down, that Chris was the guy I was describing all of those summer days. But I can assure you I was absolutely clueless. Hindsight is 20/20! In my journal, I wrote that I would be really excited if my future spouse was a drummer. So much for having a bad attitude about my housing assignment, right?

Occasionally, we have conversations about our meeting and falling-in-love story, and we both try to force our brains to remember what it was like to view each other as just a platonic friend. We've been unsuccessful, clearly, because I guess we're in love. Maybe we should stop trying to do that. Ha! But the point is that it blindsided us, and we loved it.

2

Marriage

We dated for nine months before getting engaged, and then we set our wedding date for two days after college graduation, which meant we had about a nine month wait ahead of us. We did not love engagement. I've never been one to go crazy daydreaming about the details of my wedding. This ended up being a great thing for my mom as I am the only girl in a family with three boys. If she wanted to plan a dreamy wedding for one of her children, I was the one for whom she could do it! It worked out perfectly as she is the ultimate do-it-yourselfer, and I was busy studying.

Engagement felt like a long, never-ending time period, and that feels funny to say now as we approach our fifth year of marriage. Nine months seems like no time at all, but I will never forget the anticipation and excitement mixed with the frustrating feeling that our countdown to marriage moved along so slowly. We didn't live together before marriage, and we were so looking forward to returning from our honeymoon and moving into our first apartment together.

Our first year of marriage was legitimately amazing. In fact, marriage has gotten more amazing as time has gone on. I don't mean that to sound proud or ungenuine. Having a blissful, relatively conflict-free marriage came relatively easy, but I don't mean that marriage itself is easy. We argue just like everybody else. But we always felt that life together would be far better than life apart. Keeping that perspective would end up being crucial to how we got through the next couple of years together. At the time, I didn't know why it all felt so much easier than what I had heard.

For whatever reason, we didn't experience a lot of the "newlywed shock" we had heard and read about in our premarital counseling books. Marriage has always just felt right to us. Now, I assume it was God's grace and mercy to prepare us to step into the next phase of our life unified and without a rocky foundation, but I suppose I'll never truly know. We can honestly say that looking back, we argued way more before we were married. A lot of our pre-marital arguments focused around frustrating situations that occurred because we weren't married yet. (i.e. physical boundaries, planning time to see one another in the midst of crazy schedules, and the inability to live together, etc.) We had always been really honest with one another about our hopes, dreams, fears, and desires, and we always felt like God had given us such a heart of unity for our purpose as a family. We argued, of course, but we really felt that we adjusted smoothly from non-married people to married ones.

I was still in school our first year of marriage, so I was very much still living in college mode. My only job was to attend class and do my work. Chris eventually got a job, and his hours were not the typical nine-to-five, so our schedules actually worked pretty well together. We spent our time hanging out with friends, serving at our church, cooking, working, and swimming in the pool outside of our apartment unit. It was basically the perfect situation.

3

We're Pregnant!

A large part of our heart has always been for family and children. Ever since I was very young, I've wanted to be a mom, and I have never had a real desire for a career outside of the home. I do engage in a variety of creative endeavors on the side, but I primarily felt that my God-breathed vocation was to be a mother. This didn't mean that I was a stellar babysitter, the nannying type, or someone who always gravitated towards other people's children, but rather that my affections towards my future children were already established long before Ellie made her appearance into our lives. My plan for family always included adoption.

I still remember being so excited when I found out early on in our relationship that Chris was also fond of having adoptive children. We both come from big families, so we have always envisioned ourselves with multiple children. We also felt that our desire for a large, diverse family was confirmed by God. Almost every time we received prayer from strangers, they would sense that we were "having-children kind of people" and that our ministry would be marked with the nurturance of little ones. I just knew deep down that my career would be one that revolved around raising children at home, fostering children, and adopting children. I felt that this desire was confirmed further by the fact that God had led me to a spouse who desired the same. I was so grateful. It wasn't much of a surprise when, after just a year and a half of marriage, we found out we were pregnant. I had just begun working as an investigator for Child Protective Services, so I was slightly overwhelmed by the thought of having to tell my co-workers and employers so soon! I knew the hardest challenge would probably be that infamous first trimester, considering the fact that jobs in social services are notorious for being non-stop busy. I was right. It was hard. I was sick often, dead tired, and spending my days in and out of houses riddled with horrible odors from neglectful living conditions (not the best situation for a pregnant person with a heightened sense of smell). I came face-to-face daily with families in the midst of drug addictions and abusive situations towards their children. It was emotionally challenging, for sure, but it became physically challenging because of the little one growing rapidly in my womb. Chris had chosen to go back to school to get a second bachelor's degree, and so he entered into an extremely fast-paced, accelerated nursing program at the college just down the road from my work. He would agree with me when I say that the following months were a foggy blur most of the time, but we made it through that first trimester with a lot of ginger and herbal tea concoctions (from Chris) and a lot of crying (from me). I'm still not terribly fond of the taste of ginger due to the frequency in which I had to consume it! We both settled into our new and busy schedules, and although my work was very challenging, I felt called to it. I felt that any job that allows you to offer protection to hurting children is so worth the emotional strain and the long hours. I remember thinking constantly that if I was feeling such pain just being exposed to these situations, even for a few months at a time, I couldn't imagine what these sweet children were experiencing. My heart grew more and more for orphan care through this job. I also realized just how amazing my childhood was by comparison. I called my parents often during my time in that crazy field of work to tell them how grateful I was that my childhood was marked by love, commitment, and all good things! Chris and I managed to maintain a peaceful home, and still have fun in our limited time off. Things were going really well for us as we approached the spring of 2013. Before I knew it, I was twenty-weeks pregnant, and we were so excited to find out our baby's gender. We had been enrolled as patients at a lovely little birthing center in the upstate of South Carolina. The twenty-week scan would only be our second ultrasound of the pregnancy thus far. Our first one was at eight weeks, just to verify that we were pregnant. We drove to the ultrasound imaging office and had a relatively negative experience because of the staff there. I would consider us pretty easy-to-please people, but I found myself with an exposed belly and an under-trained ultrasound technician in a room that appeared to be dual-purposed for storage. During our hour there, multiple staff members would come in and out without warning. When one of the managers saw that our technician was taking too long, she aggressively took over scanning, and then flippantly typed "GIRL" on the ultrasound screen without saying a word to us. My heart immediately jumped with excitement, but I was also aggravated that I was finding out our first child's gender in such a nonchalant way. I said, "Wait. So my baby is a girl?" And she hurriedly said yes and continued moving forward. Totally not the way I thought I was going to find out the gender of my first child. She made a passing comment as she finished that they "really don't like to do these scans before twenty weeks gestation because they are too small to see clearly", which confused me because I knew that I was twenty weeks pregnant. I could barely get out the words that I was, in fact, twenty weeks pregnant and then asked quickly if I should be worried about my seemingly off pregnancy dates. You can imagine how confusing this appointment was for us, being our first twenty-week ultrasound ever and not knowing what to expect. In response to my question about being worried, she said "No," and we were on our way. I felt very unsettled upon leaving and chalked it up to a grumpy staff and an untrained ultrasound technician. I tried not to worry what they said about her size because she assured me it was nothing to be concerned about. I had never done any of this before, so I truly didn't know what to expect. I dropped Chris off back at school and headed to work, forcing a smile and trying to give the staff at the ultrasound clinic the benefit of the doubt as I told my co-workers that we were having a girl. I settled back into work and as the stress of the experience wore off, a great excitement settled in that this little baby was a girl. It didn't take me long to begin daydreaming of naming her and meeting her and seeing her daddy hold her for the first time. Clearly this was not the most dreamy ultrasound experience, but I wasn't going to let it get me down. I looked forward to the next ultrasound so that I could see her again. Along with baby dreaming comes name picking, and

Chris and I agree that naming children is important. We didn't want to choose names for our children based on names we just liked the sound of; we were intentional about looking up meanings and praying about names that "fit" them. After that ultrasound appointment, we ended up naming our daughter Ellie Rae, Ellie meaning "bright shining light" and Rae coming from a name that means "lamb." We really got the sense that Ellie was this little fireball of a personality, as crazy as that sounds considering we hadn't met her outside the womb. Chris liked to joke that she was probably going to be pretty feisty like her mom. I'm still not sure if that was a compliment or not.

4

Ellie

I can honestly say that up until this point, the day of March 13, 2013, was one of the very worst days of my life. I was finishing up at work for the day and Chris happened to be in my office as we were going to ride home together. I received a call from my midwife who had just been sent our ultrasound images and called me from what sounded to be her car. When I heard her voice, I knew something was not right. She went on to tell me that there was "definitely something wrong" with our baby, and that her jaw, brain, and possibly heart appeared to have some major issues. I can't describe what it felt like to hear that news. Chris knew from my face and instantaneous weeping that something was very wrong. I listened on while trying not to become physically ill. As she spoke, I envisioned my baby spending months in a hospital NICU. In my mind's eye, I pictured her with severe disabilities that would rob her of a normal life. The news about a potential diagnosis didn't affect my love for her in any way. I felt nothing but intense affection towards her as I began to shift my perspective to life with a disabled child rather than life with a healthy child.

Our midwife told us she would call the maternal fetal specialists in a city nearby to set us up for an appointment. She was able to pull some strings and get us in the very next day. At this point, I assumed that our daughter's condition was serious, but I didn't know how serious. My mom drove up to meet us at the hospital the next morning.

We watched and waited in devastation as the ultrasound technician at the specialist's office completed another anatomy scan without saying much at all. The technician left to get the doctor. I could barely breathe. I held my mom's hand and stared straight into the light above my bed in sheer disbelief that this was actually happening. When the doctor came in, he confirmed that there was something seriously wrong with our baby. He began listing off the various parts of her body that appeared problematic. My whole world came crashing down as one word and one word only stuck out in the midst of the conversation: fatal.

I know now what an out-of-body experience feels like. My body was doing everything in its power to protect my mind and body from trauma. I felt every awful emotion imaginable, as well as an extreme numbness. I don't remember much of what the doctor said after I heard that word, but I can honestly say that if it were possible to die of heartache, I would have left this earth right then and there. I didn't know it was possible to experience that much heartache. I loved this child more than myself already, and a man I have never met before is standing in front of me telling me she is terminally ill.

Was this doctor really telling me that my first child would not be living on this earth with us outside the womb? Was this really happening? It all felt like a dream. A nightmare. But I knew it wasn't because I'd never felt pain like this in my dreams. He was a very sweet man and was gentle with us as he talked about some possible conditions that came to mind for which we could test. We decided to go ahead and let him perform an amniocentesis test to find out. He was "almost one-hundred-percent certain" that her condition was an almost always fatal one called Trisomy 18. This was not a condition of which I had ever heard. I searched my mind with the hope to remember anyone I could talk to who had walked away from a twenty-week ultrasound this way. There wasn't a single person I knew. I felt so alone in my shock.

We drove straight from the hospital to my parents' house, which was about an hour and a half away. I maintained some level of composure until we walked in and my dad silently embraced me with a look of such heartache on his face. Our world seemed to be spinning out of control. I got some time off work, and we spent the next few days painfully awaiting our test results. When the doctor called, he told us that our daughter did not have Trisomy 18 or Down syndrome. He also expressed that he was very surprised. I can't lie when I say that my heart so badly wanted to believe that she was miraculously healed already, and that they would find her to be perfectly healthy at our next scan. The doctor then told us that the sample he took during the amniocentesis test would be further analyzed for a variety of other genetic abnormalities. This would take days. Tear-filled conversations with friends were had, prayer sessions were held, and I returned to work with a mind full of confusion and anger.

When we finally got our extended results in, we found out that there was no trace of any genetic abnormality! At this point, I was desperate to take this as a sign that she was healed, or at least better than before. I thought that surely she must be well, considering this doctor was so confident that he would find a diagnosis of Trisomy 18. We celebrated this news with friends, and looking back, I am so glad we did. It was the only real celebratory party she'd ever get to have on earth.

We returned to the doctor at the beginning of April for another anatomy scan. I was extremely nervous, but very hopeful considering the results of the tests. To our dismay, the scan resulted in the same news. She wasn't growing as she should be, and she still had the same problems in her jaw, brain, and joints. The prognosis did not look good. The doctors told us that, while the test results came back negative, there were so many other possibilities for chromosomal abnormalities that could only be detected through very extensive testing. I began learning all I could about what they told us, and was overwhelmed by the fact that it didn't look like we would be getting a clear answer. The doctors continued to tell us week after week that Ellie would likely not make it full term, and would most likely pass away in the womb at any moment. They said that, even if she did make it to forty weeks, she certainly would be unable to live outside the womb.

It took Chris and me a while to gather our composure after such terrible news, but at some point we were able to make the decision that we would fight this in prayer. We weren't exactly sure how to go about doing this, as neither of us had ever had to pray over a life-and-death situation. But, we began praying for her health often and surrounding ourselves with family and friends who would do the same. I don't ever remember having many discussions about our theology as it relates to healing, but we sort of blindly assumed that asking for her healing was our only option.

We had plenty of people tell us that surely what Ellie had, whatever she had, was "for a reason." This never sat well with us, but we didn't do a lot of investigating as to why it felt so wrong in our hearts. We both knew and loved the Lord, and we felt that we knew His character to be one of goodness, even though we proceeded in our prayers with a lot of confusion. I remember never blaming God for what was wrong with Ellie, but rather asking a lot of "why" questions.

When I recall this time, I remember being offended quite a lot at the things people would tell us about our baby. Although she was sick, my motherly affection for her grew and grew. I felt so protective of her and so in love with her. I wasn't okay with being told that she (and her condition) were "chosen for us" for a specific reason. It made me sick. Each day was a challenge as I came face-to-face with mothers and fathers within my job who willingly abused (and even killed) their children. Here I was, as healthy as ever, with a death sentence looming over my daughter, while mothers who abused drugs throughout their pregnancies gave birth to relatively well children. In my prayers to God, I would cry out for the children in my cases, and I admit that bitterness grew in my heart regarding the injustice of our situation--especially as it related to my profession.

Throughout this confusing time, we returned to the maternal fetal specialists every other week or so. Each time we left with the defeating message that nothing had changed. Ellie was growing, but very, very slowly, and no progress was being made in terms of her abnormalities. Her jaw was significantly recessed back, her stomach bubble wasn't growing or large enough (due to the inability to swallow), her cerebellum was even further behind in growth than her body, and her hands, fingers, and feet were contracted inward. Each time we went in for an ultrasound and received news of her progress, we would send out a mass email to a group of friends and family who prayed hard for healing until our next appointment. The days and weeks went on like this as we learned exactly what it was like to be forced to lean on the strength of God, and not our own. To be honest, I know that sounds clichéd. In the face of such a traumatic pregnancy I didn't even know what it meant to lean on God and not myself. I just knew I had to keep breathing.

I can't describe to you the level of desperation I felt for the Lord each day when I woke up, but I had never experienced such a thing in my life. It opened my eyes to the fact that, when things were going well in my life, I definitely seemed to "coast" in my relationship with Him. I tried not to beat myself up for this, as I had never been faced with a situation that would show me otherwise.

But, I began to realize that no matter what happened with Ellie, I never wanted to lose this deep sense of need for Him. He was the only thing getting me through each hard hour. He was the only thing that sustained me and enabled me to sleep at night. I remember telling Him more times than I could count that I genuinely believed I would stop breathing if He didn't continue to breathe His breath into my lungs in this time of great heartache. I needed Him that bad. I need Him that bad.

Each day was truly a challenge. Every dream I had ever had of a shower for this baby was ripped from my palms. Shopping for her clothes, setting up her nursery, picking paint colors and decor, putting together a birth plan that involved us taking her home; each day I woke up pregnant and tempted to believe that it would all go back to normal. It's completely unnatural for a mother to have to rewire her brain and prepare to not bring the child that's growing in her womb home with her. When you're faced with news like this, the impulse to "nest" doesn't go away. Everything about my body was preparing me for motherhood. My instincts were to prepare and to protect and to anticipate raising this little one. I just couldn't get used to the idea that none of it would be happening the way it's supposed to.

5

Ellie's Birth

As the days and weeks moved on, this level of stress and anxiety and trauma became the norm for us. I had forgotten what it was like to *not* be staring into the face of her death sentence, although I prayed each day that she would live. It's sort of a sick feeling when you become used to tragic circumstances. I knew that if I didn't attempt to find normalcy in the midst of it all, I would lose myself. We eventually found peace in the midst of this valley, and we eventually found laughter. Don't get me wrong, there were awful, dark days of tears in the midst of it all. But we prayed over Ellie, recited Scripture over her, and talked to her about the things that were happening around her. We often laughed about the fact that she was so comfortably unaware of this great battle happening around her. I would jokingly tell her not to worry about it with things like, "We totally have this under control." I didn't have anything under control.

As we got closer to our due date, we were faced with so many hard decisions about how we wanted her birth to look. We tried hard to hold these conversations in balance with the belief that she may indeed be healed at the end of it all. But we had to have the hard conversations nonetheless with doctors who were very positive she would die. We began to laugh (with fists raised) after our appointments where the doctors would come in and be "surprised that she is still alive." Chris and I attributed it to the feisty personality she obviously got from her mother.

Although we had originally intended on having a natural birth at the birthing center, we were no longer able to give birth there due to her condition. We were planning to have a natural birth in hospital, but because her condition appeared to be so rare, we wanted to ask the advice of the specialists. We were told that having a cesarean section delivery may increase her chance of survival by a slight percentage, as she wouldn't have to endure the trial of labor. Although I did not want to have major surgery, we felt that this option was the most responsible and honoring to Ellie if it meant any percentage at all of an increased chance of survival. I was not happy about this decision. But things were so out of control that I admit it felt even just a little comforting to make my own decision about when we would deliver her. In the span of a few months, I went from thinking I would have a perfect birthing center delivery to realizing not only would I have major surgery as part of my birth story, but I'd also not be bringing my child home, barring a miracle.

The hospital was about an hour away from our home, and on the day we drove in for our c-section, we literally drove into a rainbow the whole way. My mom and dad were driving in from another direction and our dear friend Sarah was following behind us, and I got phone calls from each of them about the rainbow we were all driving towards. I am not exaggerating when I say that it seemed to be arched over the hospital. We had so many people praying for us, and I felt so much peace. I had this feeling deep down in my spirit at that point that Ellie would not be staying here on this earth with us. But, somehow I was not afraid.

All the while I continued praying for a miracle, and with as many people as we had praying for us, I felt a surreal and incomprehensible sense of calm. I was excited to meet her. I was scared to meet her, but I couldn't wait to see her face. I remember joking around with my anesthesiologist as the lower half of my body went numb from the epidural. I remember that, although the surgery scared me, nothing else did. I have this vivid memory of staring directly into

Chris' bright green eyes during surgery and thinking over and over again how much I loved his eyes and how much comfort they brought me. I told him to tell me stories to distract me from the sounds of surgery, and he began telling me stories of adventures we would have together in tropical places.

Chris is seriously a wonderful man. I realize that none of this sounds like what should be happening during this sort of delivery, but to be honest, it's one of the craziest experiences of tangible peace I've ever known. When I look back on it all, I don't feel that peace--but in that moment, it was real. I knew we were being cared for. I knew we were being prayed for.

I finally heard them say that she was out of the womb. She was rushed over to a table that I could not see due to the surgical sheet hanging in front of me. A neonatal team surrounded her, and I listened as I heard them try to intubate her and sustain her heart with epi-pens. We told the doctors previously that we did not want to put her on life support, but that we wanted her to be assessed just in case her prognosis had changed. After I was stitched up, the head neonatal doctor came to my bedside and told us that Ellie wasn't going to make it. She asked if I wanted to hold her, and I said yes.

They brought Ellie to me and placed her on my chest. My affection towards her was indescribable. I knew she was dying, and I was absolutely devastated, yet I was so happy to see her sweet, round cheeks and to hold her body against my chest. She was so gorgeous and I was so in awe of her presence. She was stunning and perfect, even though her body was not well. I now know the feelings mother's feel when they see their child for the first time, but I do not know those feelings apart from the pain and devastation that was intertwined with them. How was my heart feeling such love and pride and awe and at the same time feeling as though it was being ripped right out of my chest? I felt the tangible perfection of a mother's love and at the same time as if I would die at any moment from the pain. I spoke to her and told her that I loved her so much, and that I knew that she was already on her way to meeting Jesus face-to-face. I felt the entire spectrum of human emotions during the next few hours with her. One that stands out to me was pure jealousy that she was meeting Jesus instead of us.

We decided to keep her for about four hours, and were able to bathe her, dress her, and have pictures taken of her. This time was so surreal. I really believe that this was because of the army of people we had praying for us. Our friend Sarah stayed in the room with us, and I remember her telling me she felt the same. We had some of our family come in and see her, and then we spent the rest of our time with her by ourselves.

I have to admit that, once we said our final goodbyes to Ellie, a relief passed over me. I had this deep sense of closure and gratitude that I could rest in the known rather than the confusing time of pregnancy and anticipation. There was so much unrest in the waiting. There was deep grief and deep heartache, but I felt that I could finally enter into the process of healing. To be brutally honest, the main reason I was ready to say goodbye to her body was that I could no longer bear the fact that her body was growing colder. It was too sobering.

We were moved to a room away from the floor we were on as the hospital staff wanted to make sure we didn't have any exposure to laboring mothers and new babies. I was thankful and also devastated that we were moved. I desperately wanted to return home as soon as possible, but we had to stay for a couple nights to ensure that I was recovering appropriately from my c-section. I couldn't stand the thought of returning home without her, but I wanted to sleep in my own bed.

I had no idea how I was going to plan a funeral for my daughter, but I knew we needed to. I could barely fathom how I would survive the five minutes in front of me, much less handle the emotional strain of funeral arrangements. Our friends literally swooped in and handled so much of this for us. They faced our pain head on and dove into planning a celebration that would honor Ellie's life.

We found an amazing property of land that has been turned into an eco-burial ground, and our friends constructed a beautiful little casket for her. We painfully picked out a plot of ground down a beautiful trail in the woods on the land. We buried her between three beautiful dogwood trees. We constructed her funeral as a worship service and told everyone to wear colorful clothes to celebrate our Bright Shining Light of a daughter. It really was a beautiful time of fellowship. Challenging, but beautiful.

I want to include my original blog post about Ellie's birth story here, because it was written less than ten days after her birth and death. There is something about reading these words that takes me back to that moment, and reminds me of the little details I would have otherwise forgotten. I wrote this on June 27th, 2013.

"Ellie's Birth Story, June 27th, 2013 7:10 AM

There are really no words to do any of this situation justice. No words to describe how much we miss Ellie. No words to describe the difficulty of holding our Ellie as her heart stopped beating. I didn't want to wait too long to post simply because I don't want to forget any details, and I also want to honor those of you that have spent the past months (almost a half a year, actually) praying for our sweet girl and family. I know I've said this before, but it truly does feel like we've walked through this as a large family--we have cried with so many friends and at times it felt like we were burdening the lives of nearly everyone around us with constant devastating news .... but man, what a picture of community the way God intended for it to be. I could (and I'm sure I will) talk more about that in the future ... there's just so much. I woke up on Tuesday, the 18th, feeling sorta weird. I'm sure a lot of it was normal 38 week pregnancy weird, because I don't think there's such a thing as feeling physically "normal" at 38 weeks pregnant. So that aside, I started to leak a bit of my water, but it wasn't gushing out or anything...and I was losing a bit of my plug (for you squeamish people, this is as bad as it gets for this post.) We decided to call our doctor just to talk with him and let him know what my body was doing. He happened to be out of town in NC, but he talked with us for a while and Chris began asking him one more time about what we should do (regarding our birth plan) as we had previously been throwing around the idea of the c-section "just in case" Ellie would survive. We knew the prognosis was poor, but we began to weigh the pros and cons ...and as a mother I began to question whether or not my strong opposition to a c-section was due to fear and the desire to better "control" future pregnancies (i.e. how a c-section might affect future deliveries, scarring, etc.) I don't think there was a strong right or wrong decision here. We just wanted to be at peace either way. We really wanted a natural delivery, but we also wanted to set ourselves up for the most guilt-free scenario. I began feeling that if we had a natural delivery and she didn't make it I would wonder if a c-section could have made a difference. Some of this was spiritual attack, and some of it was just longing to make a decision that would be conducive to healing and peace of mind and heart. The doctor spoke gently and very personally with us, stating that if we were his children, he would encourage the c-section just due to the state of her body and the potential stress of labor (on her) if we waited. He told us that he wanted us to make the decision and to feel good about it, but that if we wanted to go the c-section route we would really need to go in that day (due to labor possibly coming soon and to optimize her chance of survival.) We got off the phone, talked about it, and felt very much at peace (yet terrified) with the decision to go ahead and go in. We called him back and told him and then he set everything up for us via telephone to the hospital. I had already eaten lunch, so we had to schedule for more than 6 hours from the time I had eaten, which put us at about 8:30 for scheduling purposes. We packed up a little bit and did random stuff 'til it was time to leave ... and it *was sort of surreal from that point on. Our lovely (understatement) friend, Sarah, came with us, as she was originally going to be coming with us to the birthing center from way back before we knew that Ellie had some health issues. When all of that unfolded, we felt that we still really needed her ...maybe even now more than before--just to be a rock and a prayer warrior and a super peaceful presence (if you know her ... you know what I mean.) She headed over and we headed to the hospital. As we got closer, a brilliant rainbow appeared (no joke) and we literally drove into it for the last 20 minutes of the trip. My mom texted Chris a picture of it from where she was (also driving to the hospital) and then Sarah called to ask us if we saw it. I'm kind of glad both of these things happened so that we have proof, because Chris and I were in awe of how bright it was. Chris and I didn't talk about it beforehand because we were both pretty nervous and contemplative in the car ... ... but we both felt like we just kind of knew what was about to happen. And we both felt like God was just telling us, "Hey. I'm here. We're here with you." My words aren't doing this justice, but it was awesome. We got to the hospital and the poking and prodding began (as to be expected) and this was all kind of a blur. The neonatologist came in and we had to confirm what we wanted post-birth, as the plan was originally less intervention-oriented. We still didn't change our minds about life support or any of that jazz, but we did want her to be assessed for survival chances in case things looked different outside of the womb We knew were just going to have to wait and see. I don't know how many people were lifting us up in prayer at this point … but I know it had to have been a lot, because we felt so. much. peace. As they wheeled me out of the room into the O.R. (urgh, without my husband), I literally felt the presence of way more than just two people (who were pushing me) surrounding my bed. I felt just swarmed, literally swarmed, with heavenly presences …. I didn't have Chris with me yet, but I felt so calm that I even cracked a joke with the anesthesiologist and he was all like, "Oh, gracious," and shaking his head while laughing at me. At that point, I was pretty sure Ellie was not going to make it. I just felt like God was there waiting (not as a grim reaper … … but beautiful Father-style, ready to wrap her up) and I was devastated but also peaceful. They numbed me, Chris got back there, and I spent the next 25 minutes or so staring into Chris' eyes while they did the surgery … and his eyes kept me so grounded. I told him to "talk to me about good things," so he rambled on about Hawaii (which I later found out was all he could come up with at the time) and I didn't even hear anything he said but his voice and his eyes were just the most gorgeous and soothing things ever. I heard the doctor say, "She's out" but I couldn't see her yet, and I knew the NICU team was working on her. Chris stood up and looked to the corner of the room where she was while they stitched me up, and I knew she was alive then but wouldn't be alive long ... I just knew. They told us that they were keeping her heart going by using epinephrine and trying to get some tubes down for breathing, but were having trouble due to her tiny body and some malformations. I definitely knew at that point. After about 20 to 30 minutes of working on her, the doctor told us that it wasn't looking good, and so we told them we just wanted to hold her. So they brought her to us and I got to hold her skin-to-skin while she left to be with Jesus ... I don't know how long it was that she was alive on me ... she looked so peaceful the whole time. The staff gave us some time before they came over to verify that her heart had stopped beating. She was just so beautiful and had the best little cheeks to kiss. We just wept and kissed her and told her how much fun she was already having in Heaven ... and Chris just told her a million times how sweet she was. There are no words ... there are no words for how hard this was (and is), and I can't even go into more detail because the memory is too precious. Literally, I am alive right now because the Father is sustaining me ... ... because if pure heartache could kill me--this would have. Our sweet, sweet baby. He is continuing to breathe breath into our lungs and hold our hearts. They told us we could keep her for as long as we wanted, which I never thought I would have wanted to do before all of this happened. But after seeing her, I knew we needed to hold her and love her for a while. So we kept her for a good five hours or so, just staring at her and kissing her and smelling her. Sarah helped Chris bathe her since I couldn't really move from bed--and I was so content just watching her over there ... I was being loved on by the Father and it was so surreal. Don't get me wrong, the whole thing was devastating and indescribably painful, but I think it was as peaceful as it could have been, considering the circumstances. We held her and had our families come in to see us and see her before we held her a little longer and then let the staff take her. We felt a lot of closure saying goodbye to her physically. We felt devastated and heartbroken, but it just felt like it was time to give her up. There is more I could say about right now, but we're still in this place of intense heartache and also peace, all mashed into one. There is incredible pain. Incredible. And there is a lot of weeping in bed with my sweet husband. But also overwhelming moments of comfort and beautiful impressions of Heaven where she is MUCH better off than we are ... laughing and joyful all of the time. Heaven is looking so much sweeter these days, even better than before. I've talked about this before, but my own parents know exactly what it's like to lose a child, as they lost their first daughter. My dad told me a couple days after that there literally is nothing worse, and I really hope that that is true. It makes sense as God did this willingly for us which I can't even comprehend--but clearly God knows the weight of the pain and the heartache. I can honestly say already that I'm terrified to get pregnant again in the future--and I'm working on that fear with Him...but we know it's just going to take time. We are fully prepared and waiting in expectation for full healing from the Father ... we are also fully prepared and waiting in expectation for God to use this for good, because we are declaring that there will be no more joy or hope robbed from our family. We are anxiously anticipating full and complete healing for our hearts--but missing Ellie every single second. Our beautiful friend took the sweetest pictures of Ellie, but I'm not ready to post all of them yet...so I'll do just one for now. Please continue to keep our family in your prayers as we move forward...once again, I cannot express enough gratitude for all of the prayers and love."*

6

Comfort and Mourning

In the following months, I was truly honored to get to experience the radical emotional healing God brought to us. I heard story after story of parents who would fall away from one another, divorce, or even develop mental illnesses after the loss of a child. But in just a few months, I experienced a kind of deep emotional healing that might have taken months without the Lord.

In mid-September, just three months after Ellie's death, I traveled with a few friends to a prayer training conference that happened to be at my home church just four hours away. It was the church I grew up in, and I was so comfortable there. So when I found out that this was the location of the prayer conference, I knew I wanted to attend.

During the weekend we learned all sort of techniques and tools to use when interceding for people. During different teachings we would use some basic prayer training tools on ourselves. I was definitely in an okay place emotionally during this conference, but I wasn't fully myself. I wondered if I would ever feel free-spirited and joyful again like I did before our traumatic pregnancy and loss of Ellie, or if this had forever changed me for the worse. I knew deep down that God can take any and all bad situations and use them for good. I just wasn't sure of what that would look like.

After one session ended, the staff running the conference created a prayer line we could each move through and receive some brief intercession. At this point in my life, and in the grieving and healing process, I jumped at every chance I could to receive prayer. I moved through the line once and felt blessed by the prayer. But I knew when I exited the line that my heart wasn't fully open and receptive to what God wanted to do in me. I was completely to blame as I had unintentionally built up walls of distrust towards God, and I know now that God used that first pass through the line to show me that this was true.

I believe that in the grieving process, we have so many subconscious thoughts and feelings that can only surface when prompted by another circumstance. Losing a child is such a complicated experience. I could have told everyone the "right answers" about my relationship with God and about my view of Him as my Father and Sustainer. But there were so many hidden lies that I had begun to believe out of the sheer inability to work through all of these emotions on my own.

I decided at that moment that I would enter the line again, and that this time I would be one-hundred-percent open to receive from the Lord. As the first couple of people (strangers to me) interceded for me, they began speaking about loss and grief. These people did not know me or my situation. They talked about how God saw me and how He saw the loss I had experienced. This alone was so simple, yet so necessary, for me to hear. It can be easy in times of trauma to get this sense that God is off tending to other things, and has forgotten you for the time being. You can tell yourself through a knowledge of Scripture that this is certainly not true, but I needed these words to be spoken directly to my heart. God was recognizing this lie that was so far down in my spirit, and reminding me that He was there each step of the way.

I moved on through the line to the next set of people, who began to pray grief and depression away. They began speaking to the deepest hurt in my heart, the deepest longing to raise my daughter here on this earth, and I felt the depression and grief lift off me.

I moved through the line once more, and another set of strangers began speaking prayers of comfort over me. I no longer remember what they prayed as I was swept into this extremely vivid vision in my mind's eye. I was suddenly in an area of space that was pure white, and in the center was a large chair, and Jesus was sitting in it. I looked to the bottom of the chair, and I saw myself on the floor, with my face to the ground and my body wrapped around one side of the chair. Suddenly, I was no longer watching as a third party but had entered into the scene as myself on the floor. God spoke to my heart and showed me (without words) that this situation was my current posture of grieving. I immediately realized what He was saying. I was recognizing at this stage of my life that God was indeed with me, but I was not allowing Him to comfort me to the fullest degree. I was there with him, acknowledging His presence in my life, but just out of reach.

Finally, God said to me, "You are so close. Why don't you crawl up into my lap?" I don't know how comfortable you are with the prophetic words, but the next thing that happened truly pierce my heart with love. As this played out in my mind's eye, I looked up and began to crawl into the lap of Jesus when the woman who was physically praying for me on my right-hand side said out loud, "Jesus just wants you to crawl up, right into his lap." I knew that these words in the physical were confirmation of what God was doing spiritually, and I am so grateful for the gift of discernment and that this woman was bold enough to speak what she felt in her heart. Her words solidified what He was speaking to my heart. Her words solidified that the Lord saw me and wanted to hold me in my grief.

When the prayer session ended, I left the line with more laughter and joy than I had experienced in a long time. In light of the heaviness of what we had been experiencing for months on end, I had forgotten what it felt like to laugh until my stomach hurt. My friends saw me and laughed with me, knowing that God had touched me deeply. I am not kidding when I say that those brief moments with the Lord did more in my heart and mind in the healing process than years of counseling could have done. In fact, I couldn't wait to get back home to tell Chris about it.

What is so interesting is that, in this time of prayer, I never felt pressure from God to not be sad about Ellie. He touched my heart without denying the fact that losing a child is a terrible thing. I was reminded of the verse in Matthew about how we are blessed when we mourn, because it puts us in a place where God is able to comfort us! He doesn't tell us *not* to mourn because we have no reason to; he tells us that *when* we mourn, we will be blessed by His comfort. I now know that the key component in receiving this blessing is to be receptive to it. God works in our hearts only as much as we let Him in.

7

Ellie's Little Sister

As the months moved forward, Chris graduated from nursing school, and I decided not to return to my job. I felt it would be too emotionally straining and hinder my ability to excel in working with the families and children in such hard circumstances. I honestly think child welfare jobs are some of the most emotionally challenging out there, and the benefit of doing such a hard job is certainly not financial blessing.

Chris and I talked about staying in the area and getting a job at one of the local hospitals, but we felt that we wanted a change of scenery after such a hard year. We knew that the field of nursing has so many job opportunities and is so flexible, that we could almost go anywhere. Together we decided that we would move to Charleston, South Carolina, which is where I grew up. Charleston is an amazing place to live, and although I moved near the mountains for my college career and subsequent years, I could never get the beach out of my system. Chris didn't grow up at the beach, but he was on board with coastal living (of course!) and so in December, we moved down with just our savings and the confidence that God was going to provide a job for Chris.

We did pray about where we should go after Chris graduated, and sometimes you get really clear answers about stuff like that. In our experience, we felt a lot of freedom from the Lord about where to move during this time. We felt that he wanted us to move forward and start fresh, and I am so happy he blessed our decision to live five minutes from the beach!

Chris got called in for interviews relatively quickly, and he was offered two different nursing jobs in one day at the hospital eight minutes from our apartment. He was a new graduate and was able to choose which job he preferred! It was a huge blessing, and I was so proud of him and so thankful that God's hand was on this. He began working as a nurse, and I began doing some creative work until I figured out where I should be working.

Chris' nursing schedule was pretty sporadic; he would work three days (a minimum of twelve hours) and then have four days off in a week, but not necessarily in the same sequence each week. This made it difficult for me to determine what kind of job I should get. We wanted to place quality time together at a high priority after such a rollercoaster of a year. We knew that, if I got a normal nine-to-five job, we may only see each other for a few hours in the evening and only have one full day together each week (or maybe less). We decided that our quality time together wasn't worth risking after the year we had just had. We also wanted to talk about getting pregnant again, as it had been about six months since Ellie passed away.

I never had the thought that I would want to wait a long time to get pregnant again, but I definitely wanted to be making healthy, prayerful decisions regarding that part of our life. We got pregnant with Ellie very quickly, so I knew that the chances of us getting pregnant quickly again were high. The doctors told us after Ellie passed away that the condition she had must have been an anomaly, and that there were no signs of risk that it would happen again. We felt confident in their words; the rest was just a matter of timing. Because all of her genetic testing came back negative, we were excited to not have to battle recurrence statistics that a lot of families face after receiving a diagnosis like Trisomy 18 or other chromosomal abnormalities.

It was mid-March when we felt peace from the Lord about trying to get pregnant again. Just as I expected, we were pregnant within a week. I took comfort in the fact that we were pregnant so quickly, taking it as a sign of the amazing story of hope that would unfold before me. I was elated. I was elated and terrified. We decided that I would continue working these sort of side jobs I was doing until it became impossible to do so (my job was physically intense at the time). Then, I would plan to stay home with the baby. I didn't want to have to start a more stable or serious career and take on added responsibilities, only to tell them that I wouldn't be returning to work after the baby arrived. Staying home to parent is something we had always planned on if we could financially swing it.

I wish I could say I fully trusted God in waiting for my twenty-week anatomy scan, but I definitely struggled each and every day of the first half of the pregnancy to fight fear. I knew that the fear I was experiencing was not from God. This made it manageable to battle, but it was certainly not fun. There were many tears and anxious moments, but for the most part I had a fun time dreaming about this new life which which we had been blessed. I practiced fighting fear by recounting the words of the doctors regarding the projected health of our future children. I tried hard to do "normal" pregnancy things, like shop for clothes every now and again, and browse the aisles in the baby departments of stores, a task that should have been easier and more exciting than it was for me. It was so hard not to dream of all the sweet clothes Ellie should be wearing as she accompanied me to shop for her little sister.

We found an amazing doctor in a hospital that was walking distance from our apartment. She was so kind and gentle with us as we related our experience with Ellie to her. We were treated with such honor every time we went in for our ultrasounds. I got a plethora of ultrasounds this time around, which was a far cry from the way we started our pregnancy with Ellie. I wanted peace of mind, and they wanted to provide us with it. I got an ultrasound at six weeks, eight weeks, twelve weeks, and sixteen weeks, and everything looked great. I was becoming more and more confident about this pregnancy, and I was already falling in love with this baby.

At our sixteen-week appointment, we found out that this baby was also a girl! We were so excited. I dove headfirst into the world of baby-naming. I had already picked out several that I loved. I often pressured Chris with my list of "names with awesome meanings" and he, being the patient man that he is, listened to me. But he also offered that "it has to feel really right." I began praying that God would provide the perfect name, and I even prayed that he would give it to Chris, and not me, so that he could be even more confident in naming her.

Sure enough, Chris left to attend a worship-and-prayer night at our church and, although we normally would go together, I stayed home because I wasn't feeling that great. When he left I thought, "I wonder if he is going to get a name." That may sound totally weird, but I had this crazy feeling that it was going to happen. I absolutely believe in swiftly answered prayers, but I'll admit I was a little bit shocked when Chris came home and said, "I heard a name during worship!" I asked him what it was and he said, "Elsie."

At first I was a little taken aback because the name was so similar to Ellie, but I grabbed my phone to search the name Elsie and announced the disclaimer that, if it had a weird meaning, we definitely couldn't use it, and for him to please not be discouraged if this was the case. I actually loved the name Elsie as soon as it left his lips, but I wasn't getting my hopes up. I pulled out my phone and researched the name, and tears began to stream down my face when I saw what it meant. Chris was staring, waiting for me to tell him. I said, "It's perfect. It means 'My God is Abundant' or 'God of plenty.'" Chris' eyes teared up and we hugged. We were so happy that we had the most perfect name for our redemption baby. We don't know anyone named Elsie and it had never crossed my mind as I put together my list of favorites, but the fact that it combined Ellie's name with such a profound meaning was confirmation that it was right for her.

I had previously dreamt that Noelle was part of

her name. It didn't occur to me until later that this makes perfect sense to use, because it literally means "name given to children born at Christmas". Her due date was December 23rd. I'm not usually one for loving familiar holiday-type baby names, but in my dream I was so sure of it. Her name was officially Elsie Noelle. Little did I know that I would end up going into labor on Christmas night. Elsie Noelle. My God *is* abundant.

8

Twenty Weeks

I was nervous, yet excited, for our anatomy scan at twenty weeks because I knew that I could finally put all of this anxiety to rest with the medical proof that all was well. Our appointment was in August. We had a ton of people praying for our hearts to be at peace for this appointment. We watched closely, and I smiled as I saw each part of her wiggly body. I tried to pay close attention. We had been to so many ultrasounds with Ellie that I knew what to look for.

Suddenly, our ultrasound technician turns to us and says, "When is your due date again?" I wasn't sure what she meant by this question, but I assumed she had our dates down wrong in the computer system. I told her it was on December 23rd, and then she said, "Oh, that's so weird, because she's measuring about three weeks off." I absolutely died inside when I heard these words. In fact, as I type this, words can't do

justice to express the panic and terror Chris and I felt.
I don't quite know how to describe these moments. I
felt utter hopelessness. I felt the complete death of this
dream. Everything I had dreamt about our miracle,
redemption baby was gone. I was left with nothing
to grasp and no way to wake myself up from this
nightmare that I knew was beginning again. I begged
and pleaded silently to Jesus that the technician
alluded to her being three weeks *bigger* rather than
smaller, which would mean we got pregnant earlier
than we originally thought. But then I remembered
that the earliest ultrasounds are the most accurate,
and we were sure our estimated due date was correct.
I knew in that moment that we would be reliving the
devastation we had just walked through with Ellie.

She finished the scan and then told us she would
be right back with the doctors. As soon as she left the
room, shock settled in, and Chris and I sat in dead
silence. Chris was in such shock that I remember his
head nodding in and out of a trauma-induced sleep.
It was terrible to see. Of all that we have walked
through together, the memory of seeing him in that
state still makes me feel sick. He couldn't remain with
me emotionally because he was struggling, as I was,
to not be fully overcome by the news we were hearing.
I don't remember moving any part of my body for
the next twenty minutes or so. I stared into the grey
wall in front of me, wondering if I would wake up

from the nightmare I was experiencing. I can tell you everything about that wall in front of me. Every crack. Every groove and dent. The image of that room is forever engraved upon my mind. Moments that felt like years passed until finally the technician returned with a doctor.

We had gone to a different imaging center for this ultrasound than our eight-week ultrasound, so the staff did not know us or our story. They began telling us the very same things we had heard at our first horrible appointment with Ellie. It sounded like a broken record as he described the exact same characteristics that Ellie had. I somehow uttered the words, "This happened before." And then we attempted to fill them in on Ellie's condition. I was an absolute and total wreck. Again, I don't even know if I can adequately describe what the next few minutes felt like. I felt like my heart was being ripped straight from my chest, and that my lungs would certainly forget to do their job. I texted Sarah, and all I could manage to say was "It's the same," to which she responded with one word: "No." I stared at that small word, trying to agree with the "No". No, this cannot be. I cannot do this again.

We were taken to another small room where a genetic counselor attempted to get as much history as she could from us. But we knew already that there was nothing in either side of our families that would imply a predisposition for any genetic abnormality. We had already walked down this road before. I knew that no words that came out of my mouth would change the outcome of what was to happen. They asked if I wanted to do an amniocentesis test, but I informed them that Ellie's tests came back completely negative. They told us we should consider terminating, and that we would need to do so before twenty-four weeks gestation. As much as I know we are against aborting, I have to be honest in saying that my heart felt that it would be so much easier. I almost wished I could be okay with it, just to end this pain I was experiencing. As much as we like to think that our belief systems are strong, coming face-to-face with certain situations can call into question why we believe what we do. I held on to the notion that choosing death was out of the question. But I can't say I wasn't tempted to escape this pregnancy.

Chris and I left the office and wept hysterically in the car, all the while texting just a few people to send out a mass message to everyone we knew. I had a panic attack for the first time in my life. It was horrific. That night we drove to our pastor's house and sat with him, his wife, and our closest friends as we worked back through our appointment. All I remember is having a pounding headache and an uncontrollable need to weep. It was all I could do to prevent myself from throwing up. I confessed my overwhelming desire to back out of the pregnancy and was met with loving compassion and the reminders that I needed to get my heart and mind back under control.

We, as a family and as believers, are convinced that it is our responsibility to choose life in every situation, and not only as it relates to pregnancy. When we are born again into God's kingdom, our citizenship is in Heaven. We hold the keys to life, which Jesus won back when he died and rose. This absolutely has to be the position from which we operated. I was so thankful that I could be vulnerable in front of these amazing people.

As we settled into this new reality with Elsie, we felt an extreme loss of hope for our family and our future. We felt like the promises spoken over us had once again been robbed. We had no idea how we were going to move forward.

One evening, maybe a few days after we found out this news, we had our missionary friends Evan and Alicia over for dinner. During our meal, they both asked challenging questions and listened intently to find out where our hearts and minds were in all of this. They began speaking to places in our hearts that needed to be addressed. They felt an overwhelming need to have God restore hope back into our spirits. We prayed for a long time, and all the while we were grateful to have discerning friends who were so obedient to listen to God speak over our family. Elsie's name had an entirely new meaning for me now. It was more powerful.

Although God's abundance is an incredible thing to ponder at any time in life, I knew that He had spoken his abundance over our family in an entirely different way than we imagined. We would need His abundant and merciful love to walk us through life without another one of our children.

We ended our prayer time with a burning hope and determination in our hearts that our family would fight this once again, that we would not give up, and that no matter what happened, we would not be defeated. We were reminded that Ellie's death wasn't a loss, as she was met by Jesus with open arms. The enemy may have thought he had won the battle with her, until she breathed her last breath and entered into the eternal glory of God's kingdom.

We decided that, however hard this may be, we were going to fight for Elsie's healing to be realized here on this earth. We would dive into Scripture and prayer and worship harder than ever before, and we would face this condition with power, love, and life. The first thing I remember doing was wrestling with this idea of "trials" on this earth. I remember writing this journal entry as I tried to unpack how this was:

*"One thing that God has been showing me is that it's much too easy to get caught up in a false idea of redemption here on this earth. Believing in redemption that will **certainly be seen in this lifetime** is sort of like believing in karma. Essentially, what we're saying is that when bad things happen like this to seemingly undeserving people, there MUST be good things ahead. When I say "good things," I'm talking about good life circumstances rather than the goodness of God. And THAT is where the distinction needs to be made.*

*The goodness of God **does not equal** good life circumstances, although all good life circumstances ARE a gift from God.*

*It's easy to look at our life and see what happened with Ellie and think "surely, this baby will be fine. Look at what they've been through already." But in reading Scripture...that is just not true. We were never promised a healthy baby after Ellie. We hoped for it and we do still believe that we will raise children in our home one day, **but it is not promised to us, and it is not God's fault.***

This desire for redemption and justice is not a bad thing in and of itself, but it cannot be a desire from which we operate and consequently feel that God should operate, as well. This is exactly the reason God rebukes Job's well-meaning friends in the midst of their desire to comfort Job.

Their thinking is well-meaning, but skewed. Job's friends reduced all evil to "retributive suffering," caused by disobedience and sin ... and on the flip side, they believed that surely, because Job is righteous, God will deliver him from all suffering. God ends up telling them, **"You have not spoken of me what is right like my servant Job has."** *If we actually thought the way of Job's friends, avoiding tragedies in life would be so simple. We could live righteously and fully devoted to God and be able to expect a life full of blessing and good circumstances. Easy.*

It's also important to remember that God did not cause Job's suffering, but the enemy. You may think, "Well, God still allowed it." And that is true. And I don't fully understand that part, but I do know that what is clear is that redemption has been promised to us through the means of everlasting life, not through happy endings and a life of ease (although Job was indeed blessed in his later years.)

We aren't pessimistic--we do have hope that we will experience blessings in this life ... and we already are so blessed. Just turn on the news. **I am so blessed to live in this country where I will not expect violence**

***and death to come knocking on my door because I
have written this post.*** *But the key is that we do not
demand these things of God and we do not expect Him
to operate out of our boxes of desired retributive suffering
and/or retributive blessing."*

Clearly, the book of Job is full of questions into
which theologians and pastors continue to delve. I
am certainly not claiming to have all of the answers,
especially as they apply to hardship and tragedy on
this earth. What I do know is that we can't scare God
away with our questions. He is a safe dwelling place
for us to come to, and He will not forsake us when
we seek Him.

9

Elsie's Birth

The next months were a marathon of prayer sessions for her, fellowship with friends, and communion with one another. We spent a lot of time having conversations about protecting our hearts from all the things people used to say to us about Ellie. We were really careful to spend time talking with those that we knew would stand firm for our family and carry our hearts that were so fragile in all of this. Even though I knew I had experienced deep healing after Ellie, this entire process occasionally opened Ellie-related wounds in my heart. I tried hard to focus on the present, even though I spent many a moment stuck in places of deep despair. It wasn't easy, and it wasn't simple. Every day I had to make a conscious decision to get out of bed and come to the Lord in prayer. There were so many days that I truly felt like dying. I had no idea how I was going to make it through all of this.

I could write for hours about what not to say to an infant-loss parent, but one thing in particular that comes to mind as I write is how people would allude to it being easier this time around, since we had been through it before. I suppose that this concept applies to many things in life. Doing anything for the second time should be easier than the first.

This logic doesn't apply to infant loss. I would offer that this logic doesn't apply to loss of any kind. I can tell you that losing Ellie and losing Elsie were equally hard. There were aspects of each pregnancy that were different from each other, but one of the things that made pregnancy with Elsie so different was that I knew what was ahead, barring a miracle. Heading to the hospital with Ellie was scary, but I had never experienced saying goodbye to a child of mine before. With Elsie, I knew the pain and the heartache I would experience in saying goodbye again. There is no "easier" way to lose a child. There is never an easier way.

As Elsie's due date approached, we had no idea of the state of her health. We had refused further ultrasounds so that we could spend our pregnancy as peacefully as possible. We hoped for the best. I can't say that I was confident she was healed, or confident that she wasn't healed. Each day was different. I had to practice a lot of grace with myself, especially on the days when praying was exhausting. I think that, sometimes, those days are the best, because we are forced into places of surrender and stillness.

I rarely remember days of surrender that weren't accompanied by flowing tears and fits of anger. I found that there were a few friends in particular that offered themselves as human punching bags at which I could hurdle my angry thoughts. They would meet these thoughts with loads of mercy and loads of truth, without ever making me feel judged or condemned. I knew that their actions towards me were a reflection of God's heart towards me. He wanted me to come to Him with all of it. He wanted the sadness, the anger, and the heartache because He wanted to meet it with grace and mercy.

Elsie's due date was two days before Christmas, and I was really hoping she wouldn't come on Christmas day. I feared that her birthday would forever be on one of our favorite days of the year. It was hard enough getting through this holiday without the joys of writing sweet Ellie's name on presents and watching her grow into family holiday traditions. I knew that, if she didn't make it, my heart needed her birth day to be any other day but this one. But, her due date came and went. We couldn't travel on Christmas day, so we spent the day with some of our best friends. I hoped each hour she would wait a little longer to make her appearance.

I truly believe that spending Christmas day with our friends enabled me to go into labor that night, as we laughed so incredibly much! My belly ached from laughing so hard, and when we got home, I realized how sore my body was at forty weeks and two days pregnant. We arrived home at 10:30 PM and went to sleep around 11:30 PM. I woke up at 1:00 AM to a gush of water. I woke Chris up, as well, and we spent the next hour or so resting. Then, the contractions started coming at 1:30 AM. I was a bit nervous at this point, because I knew I had already been up for about fourteen hours (aside from the two hours of sleep before my water broke). I had hoped I would be well-rested for the start of labor.

The contractions were mild and about 8-12 minutes apart all night. We hoped to labor at home until I was much closer to active labor. Chris ended up calling the doctor around 8:00 AM to update him, but he wasn't too familiar with our case. He thought at first we should come in right away since my water had already broken at 1:00 AM, but once he looked over our chart and understood our situation with Elsie, he said we had the freedom to labor at home or come in. My contractions slowed down quite a bit, so at around 11:00 AM we decided to head to the hospital to be in a more medically stable environment. A big reason for this: there is a higher chance of infection the larger the gap between water breakage and birth, and my water was actually meconium stained which indicates fetal distress. But, it is also common with babies with conditions like Elsie's.

Once at the doctor, we got checked in and I was having irregular contractions that fluctuated between 3-4 minutes apart, 8 minutes apart, and back down to 3 minutes apart. The doctors were really great with us due to our situation, and we had written into our birth plan that we didn't want to do any fetal monitoring at all. We knew if she was healed everything would be fine, and that if she wasn't we wouldn't want any distress causing us to make rash decisions. This gave us so much freedom in how we labored with her, and it was wonderful. I was able to bounce on a birthing ball and walk around as I pleased, although I ended up feeling most comfortable laying on my side. My contractions were getting much stronger, but not necessarily closer together, which made it really hard for my cervix to dilate as it needed. We aren't really sure why it fluctuated so much.

Mentally, I started having a hard time when we hit the 24-hour mark since my contractions had begun and I was still only dilated to about 3 centimeters. They ended up putting a monitor on my belly to try and figure out a contraction pattern, but again, there wasn't one. The contractions weren't close enough together to make a significant difference, although they were pretty hefty contractions.

We originally intended to have a natural, med-free birth, but definitely did not anticipate the situation we would be in--that my body would end up needing pitocin to get me further along. I continued to labor naturally until the 24-hour mark, and when they checked dilation, they thought I really needed to start on pitocin to get the contractions more consistent. This was to make sure we didn't continue to risk our chance for infection. Usually they would push the pitocin much earlier, but they were so kind to us because of Elsie.

I heard how hard contractions were with pitocin, but I was definitely not prepared for how rough it was. With normal contractions, there is a sort of "wave" of pain that gets strong at the peak but then backs down. It makes it easier mentally to get through them as you can feel the rhythm of them.

My contractions on pitocin were insane. I talked with the nurses later and found out this is pretty much the norm, but pitocin contractions hit hard right away at the "peak" level and plateau at that same intensity until the end. There is no way of bracing yourself mentally for how long they will be as they don't build and release like natural contractions do. Once they hit, Chris and Alicia would run over and do natural relaxation techniques with me, but I felt like all I could think about was wondering how long it would last as there was no indicator at all during the midst of it. I was determined to labor naturally for as long as possible, even on the pitocin, and I ended up making it about six hours. Good gracious, I will never forget that pain. Around the four hour mark with the pitocin, we began talking about an epidural. By the time we had reached the six-hour mark of pitocin (still no epidural), I had been contracting for 30 hours.

During those six hours, they were upping my pitocin level every hour by 2 (mg?) and I think I got up to 18 (mg?) when I hit a real roadblock. I was so tired I couldn't even think. I had been awake at that point for over 42 hours. We got a very timely email from a friend about there being a time and a place for medication--and it honestly helped me so much. I felt like I needed to give myself a break, and it was good to hear it from all of the people I loved. We ended up deciding to go with an epidural at that point, and I felt so much peace about it. I was so happy I could experience those 30 hours of labor naturally with Elsie. I felt like I got the "experience" I wanted. As Chris told me, we didn't want to push it and then have it affect our meeting Elsie for the negative. I wanted to have a sound mind seeing her rather than being focused on the pain having ended.

I started being able to doze off between contractions

and Chris got some sleep, too. My contractions were really progressing and getting regular. At around 11:00 AM I told the nurse that I was really feeling the contractions through the epidural and wondered if that was normal, or if I was no longer getting the proper dosage. She felt like we needed to have the doctor come check me because it could mean that I was ready to push. At 11:10 AM I was checked again, and I was super surprised to hear that I was fully dilated and ready! We were so unprepared that Alicia wasn't even with us--she was a couple miles away at our house trying to grab a bit of sleep! Chris got in touch with her and she rushed over after I had pushed just a few times. I was so glad they didn't have to tell me when to push as I could feel the contractions coming. I felt very in control of the situation and it was so, so good. Alicia made it there and I pushed for about 45 minutes before Elsie made her grand (and fast) entrance.

When she came out, they placed her right on my chest, and I knew at that point that she wouldn't be staying with us for very long. The first thing I noticed about her were her big beautiful lips--a trait that I absolutely admire on her daddy! Through tears we showered her with loving words and watched as she wiggled her arms and moved her lips and blew some bubbles as she tried hard to use those little lungs. After a few minutes I knew she had left us. We wept and wept and told her how much we loved her and how jealous we were that she was with Jesus and Ellie. The team worked around me to fix me up and make sure all was well with my body.

My eyes could barely leave her. She was the most beautiful girl and I was so deeply in love with her. We gave her millions and millions of kisses. We had family and some friends come in small batches to see her and to love on us, and it was a really sweet time. After a while, we were transferred to a room in the postpartum unit and the two of us were able to snuggle her alone, starting at around 3:00 or 4:00 PM and through the night.

We didn't keep Ellie through the night when we had her, and this time we knew we wanted to keep Elsie with us. We were grateful that we could shape this experience to be just how we wanted it to be, due to the fact that we had been through it before. I ended up sleeping from 11:00 PM to 5:00 AM and when I woke up, I was so happy that I could walk over to her little bed and bring her back to bed with me.

It may seem so strange to feel happy about seeing my daughter, already deceased, again in the morning, but I longed to hold her and spend as much time as I could staring at her face and body. If you have children, you know the pride that you feel when you see them for the first time. This doesn't change for infant-loss parents. Even though her spirit had left, there was no way to turn off my pride for her as my daughter. My heart felt as though it was being ripped from my chest all the while, but I felt proud and in love as I lay with her on my chest. Chris would steal her away from me every so often, and seeing the way he looked at her made me laugh with joy and cry with heartache at the same time. I tried not to imagine what it would be like to be taking her home with us alive, as it was just too painful to bear, but I made peace with the fact that I was snuggling her physical body as long as I could, and that her spirit was already experiencing all of the most wonderful things. It felt so amazing to warm her body with mine under blankets, trying to memorize what she felt like in my arms.

In this entire experience with her, physically leaving her in the morning as we left the hospital was so much more painful than any other part, even greater than when her spirit left the earth after she was born. I knew we were just leaving her physical body-- but it was tremendously heart wrenching. We said our painful goodbyes and headed home around 9 in the morning, not even 24 hours after delivering. Leaving her was terrible. I forgot how much a heart could hurt.

10

Home Again With Empty Arms

As we arrived home without baby number two, I realized that this road of recovery was not going to be the same as before. It seemed that everything that happened with Ellie was compounded by Elsie's arrival and death. Now, we were dealing with the fact that there is likely a genetic reason as to why we cannot have healthy babies. There seemed to be an added layer of loss as I began to mourn the fact that I may never be able to carry healthy children of my own. The loss of biological motherhood is one that so many women deal with, and one that crept up on our family in such a dramatic way. I could never have imagined that this kind of infertility would be a part of my life, especially after watching both of my girls die right on my chest.

We celebrated Elsie at a beautiful ceremony that was totally different than the one we had for Ellie. I found that I couldn't imagine myself handling Elsie's funeral the same way as Ellie's. Although Elsie's pregnancy did sometimes feel like history repeating itself, Elsie was a different child with a different story in a different time and place, and we wanted to handle her life celebration as such. We celebrated her with a house packed full of our dearest friends and a view of the beautiful intercoastal waterway that runs through our town. We sang and cried and listened to a gorgeous sermon written just for her.

My brother's child was born during this time.

My nephew was born during Elsie's funeral.

My family drove from the funeral of their second granddaughter straight to the hospital to welcome their grandson into the world.

I love my nephew dearly and he is a constant reminder of life and redemption. And his parents are dear to me and their journey to him was not full of rainbows and butterflies. Their story is not mine to tell, but it was a trying year for my family as a whole. My sweet nephew's life was truly the gift we all needed, as painful as the ache in my heart was. But the sting of jealousy is one that has overtaken my mind more often than not, and it is an aspect of grief that consistently hits hard for me. Processing each new pregnancy announcement and each new healthy ultrasound and each new birth is a constant struggle.

A couple of weeks after Elsie's death, we were told that we could opt to send a sample of Elsie's blood, along with samples of ours, to a lab to be tested using an in-depth genetic sequencing process called Whole Exome. We were hopeful that, with such a detailed test, we would come out with some answers that would give us peace about the possibility--or impossibility--of having healthy biological children. It took about eight weeks to get our test back, and to our disappointment, the results were inconclusive. According to the doctors, this means we had to assume that the problem is autosomal recessive, at least. This means the chance of a recurrence rate with fatal diagnosis would be 25% each pregnancy. However, there is also the slight possibility that we suffered two anomalies in a row. There is also the possibility that the issue is mitochondrial, meaning we would receive a fatal diagnosis 100% of the time. There is honestly no way to know, aside from getting pregnant and waiting to see.

When people ask me what that means for me personally, I respond with, "What would it mean for you?" And their response is the same as mine. "I have no idea." Their gut reaction to my question is how I feel. I have no idea. I have no idea if I could willingly get pregnant again, knowing the suffering that could come from another fatal diagnosis. I have no idea if the possibility of a healthy child is worth trying to have if there is a chance it will end with another baby funeral. I don't know that my stance on this subject would be the same if we had healthy biological children intermingled within our loss. If the odds truly are a 75% chance of a healthy baby and 25% not, that means we got pretty unlucky twice. What if we had had a healthy child first, and then we lost Ellie, and then had another healthy child? This could have altered everything I have felt and feel to this day about my experience with loss. My perspective would be totally different.

But it's not. There are more questions than answers, and the world of DNA testing is constantly evolving and growing. We are absolutely open to further testing and hope that we will one day have the knowledge that will make our decision process easier. I have said multiple times to friends that, even if my chances of biological motherhood is a "no," I'd rather know that than nothing at all. The unknown certainly doesn't make it easy on our hearts. You can see how this topic makes my heart hurt when people ask about it. I want to be an open book and I wish I had a clear answer to give when friends wonder what's next for us. The sting of our story and the uncertainty of all of our testing has me waving my white flag of surrender as I mutter responses like, "Uhhhh, no clue." In case you're wondering, it's really fun to have no clue if getting pregnant will lead to the death of another child or not. It's also fun to have no clue how to describe that to those who ask.

11

Life and Marriage After Loss, Again

Life after infant loss is almost just as confusing as the pregnancies and the deliveries and the funerals themselves. So much of those time periods were marked by trying to survive that the aftershock of moving on in life without your children can feel so disorienting. Everything feels different. Everything feels tainted with sorrow.

One of the most helpful things I've experienced in all of this is connecting with other parents who have been through the same thing (or at least close to the same thing). Infant loss and infertility look like a lot of different things, but the pain is real and it is all so similar. That's one of the reasons I wanted to write about our story in general; to tell you that you're not alone. Maybe you have experienced loss yourself, or maybe you are walking closely with someone who has experienced it. There is power in numbers, even if I absolutely hate that there are multiple families out there who have experienced this awful side of life.

We wrestle daily with what it means to be strong, with what it means to be prayerful, and with how to respond to well-meaning individuals who say the very worst things. We wrestle with what our life is supposed to look like now, even though we know that parenthood is going to be a part of it. We wrestle with how to be angry in healthy ways, and how to make sure we don't stay in a place of despair.

After a few particularly rough weeks, we decided to go to grief counseling. There has been something so freeing about processing tough emotions in front of someone who is trained to understand and shed light on them. We go together because we have each processed our grief differently, as men and women tend to do. We have made a conscious and daily effort to stay connected to one another and to do whatever it takes to understand each other.

It is easy to become disconnected from your spouse or partner in the face of trauma, because we all tend to handle things so differently. This is especially true in the world of infant loss. Mothers deal with the loss of their children so differently than fathers do. We learned recently that one of the meanings of the word "grief" as it is used in scripture is literally, "the love of a mother." Pause for a moment and think about that! That is mind-blowing, yet not surprising at all. The mother's bond to her baby starts so early on. The father's bond may be present during the pregnancy, but usually doesn't translate as powerfully as the mother's until the baby is born. This means that, at the end of the pregnancy, the mother has seven or eight months more of bonding time than the father has at the time of birth. For our family, this meant that Chris was thrust into the world of mourning his child after just falling in love with her the way I had fallen in love with her many months before. When she was born, I experienced a deeper love than what I felt during the pregnancy, but the transition of my bond once my girls were born was much less dramatic than that of Chris'.

I especially remember feeling so much more of an aching sensation to have a baby in my arms after Ellie came and left. Chris was desperately trying to process all of his emotions at once. I was ready very soon after Ellie passed away to get pregnant again, and then I was ready very soon after Elsie passed away to pursue adoption. I had spent 9 months, both times, falling in motherly-love with my children, and then had them stolen away right after delivery. I knew they could never be replaced, but I longed to pursue parenthood again quickly since I had already had two pregnancies-worth of feeling that parental connection, one that Chris didn't really feel until the end.

I won't tell you how exactly we handled the timing of getting pregnant again after Ellie or how we've handled the timing of pursuing parenthood after Elsie because I think every family is different, but I will say that the key to moving forward has to come out of a place of unity. Unity can't come unless both parties can come to terms with the fact that males and females are wired completely differently, and even then, every individual in general handles grief uniquely.

Every time Chris would tell me that he wasn't ready or that he felt like I was just trying to "replace" our girls, I would immediately jump to the defense, rather than understanding that he was processing differently than me. I misinterpreted his grief and his questions and felt in my heart that he was shooting down my longing to be a mother. Women, keep in the forefront of your mind the heart and good nature of your men. It is so easy to walk forward blinded by pain. I can't tell you how many conversations about growing our family have ended in harsh words that can never be taken back merely because we failed to see that we both have the best interest of our families in mind, even if our desired paths look different.

I have talked to mothers after loss who wanted to wait years to pursue parenthood again, and others who wanted to get pregnant as soon as their bodies would allow. At the end of the day, each of us had to give the other space to vent and to process out loud, and not to make assumptions about what we thought the other was "really saying." I have learned that open-ended questions are key to understanding my husband when it comes to big life circumstances. He needs to feel free to express himself without feeling backed into a corner. And when he *does* answer my questions, he needs to know that I'm not waiting to jump to the defense.

The worst thing we could have done in our situation would have been to discontinue open dialogue. I needed to know what was going on in Chris' head, and vice versa. It was almost impossible for me to have these conversations with a level head until months after Elsie's birth. I'm still not perfect at it, but I'm getting better! When we feel like our interests or desires are getting unintentionally attacked, we have to practice pausing, asking for clarification, and then moving forward.

Something we realized in the midst of these hard conversations is that things have the tendency to stay pretty serious after events like child loss. I really think this happens because so many people are consistently asking you how you are, not to mention the reality that it's just on your mind all the time. "Serious" can naturally become the new baseline for your emotions.

For the first time in our marriage, we were having to consciously "choose" life and joy and laughter, whereas it seemed to come quite naturally before this. We used to be able to just go on a walk and talk about whatever came to mind and it would be a relaxing time, but when the thing that's on your mind is tragedy, or missing your baby, it can be helpful to think of activities to do together that force some fun into your life. After one particularly hard day we really needed an escape, so we spontaneously headed to the local indoor trampoline park and we jumped our hearts out and then planned a super delicious sounding meal to cook together.

Someone made a really good point to us that we don't have to always "escape" our worries through prayer or reading the Word. In the Old Testament, Leviticus was God's idea for entering into life and relationship with him, and Leviticus is full of tons of specific day-to-day actions people are meant to follow to set themselves apart and to commune with God. Connecting with God doesn't always looked like journaling or reading the bible or listening to a sermon; we can engage with him in a variety of ways, even at a trampoline park. We left that place feeling so uplifted and refreshed, simply by choosing to chase after the good gift that is indoor trampolining.

Our days would be quite sad if we couldn't commune with the Lord outside of reading the Bible or going to church! Think about a busy surgeon who doesn't get to sit down and read until the very end of the day, or who only gets a few quiet minutes to pray before entering a workplace that demands intense levels of concentration. His or her day can be spent in communion with the Lord simply by choosing to work with an outpouring of dedication and love.

I am not suggesting that trampoline parks are an excuse to avoid reading the Word or spending time in prayer, but the point is it's a good thing to go out and do something fun, knowing that God is all around and that his heart is for your spirit to be refreshed and renewed in healthy ways.

I think one of the most challenging components in grieving as a couple has been the fact that men have this amazing ability to compartmentalize things, in order to move forward and to press on. Chris is the sole provider for our family, and somehow he has to show up to work, keep people alive (he's a medical professional), and not be paralyzed with the emotional distraction that is the grieving process. It can be easy for women to interpret this ability as a cold, robotic, detached form of coping. But in reality, this has nothing to do with the pain and heartache Chris is dealing with inside. In fact, I have learned that this ability is truly a strength that I can rely on to get me through some of my more difficult moments. Chris has breakdowns just like I do, and we have been blessed enough to have our biggest emotional downfalls at different times, allowing the other to provide comfort and hugs and encouragement.

I honestly believe this is a beautiful picture of God's intent for marriage. We aren't supposed to experience this stuff alone. God is always there for us, and he works through our family to touch our hearts. He designed family to be a powerful support system. When we do not commit to supporting each other, we can cause more harm than good. It's okay to grieve differently. It's okay to have differing opinions about your individual experience with loss, but it's not okay to use these differences to divide you. You're in this together.

One of the most challenging aspects of walking this road of loss is that the loss of a child (or two) affects so many aspects of who we are. It affects our choices as parents, it affects our outlook on life, it affects our personality, our coping practices, our stress levels, and our marriage. We have found that when we do not actively pursue open communication regarding grief and pain, it can wreak havoc on our relationship. Many times, we have found ourselves in situations in which a season of heartache related to our girls has worked its way into areas we didn't intend for it to, and it can lead to explosions that feel "out of the blue" or random. These occurrences are a normal part of life post child-loss, but they can be avoided more effectively when we choose to "check in" with one another from time to time about our daughters. It can be wildly painful to talk about, but we know the worst thing you can do in the face of tragedy is to suppress your feelings for long periods of time. It's tempting to do so, probably more so for men than for women, but facing it all head on is worth the temporary heartache to avoid major crisis five or ten years down the road from pain undealt with.

12

Relating to God in Grief

I desperately wish I could be writing about how our daughter was miraculously healed, and how this greatly affected my theology and relationship with God, and that I started this book while I was still pregnant with Elsie and unsure of how it would all end. On the flip side, I was given book after book after book during my pregnancies about women who had been through variations of what I was going through, and each seemed to have a fairytale ending of sorts-- whether it was getting pregnant again with a healthy baby, having successful in-vitro fertility treatments, or being brought a child through adoption. Each story had a tangible sign of redemption on this earth. I don't have that yet, because it's not what our life looks like right now. I don't want to wait for a tangible sign of redemption to tell you and myself that it's going to be okay. And in the moments where everything isn't okay, that's fine too.

I absolutely long for justice, all the while knowing that I'm not entitled to anything on this earth. I have redemption because I've been redeemed. I do believe with all of my heart that I will see the goodness of the Lord while I am here in the land of the living (Psalm 27:13). It is possible that life could change drastically for us in a short period of time. We could welcome a child into our family soon, or we could continue to walk through life with just the two of us. Regardless of what happens, whether good or bad, the state of our hearts and our eternal perspective is most important.

Before I was ever pregnant, my friend Kim told me a story about a walk she took in the woods while dealing with a difficult situation. She prayed and thought and walked and searched for an answer, but wasn't having any intense revelations. It had been a while and all of the sudden the sun started to set, and she knew she didn't want to walk back to her car in the dark by herself. In the face of unanswered questions and surrendered hands, she turned around and went home. I loved that story, even before I experienced pregnancy or trauma of any kind, because it's so the opposite of what we want to hear. We want to hear that she walked into the woods with questions and came out with answers in the form of a holy epiphany. But instead it got dark, so she left.

We live in such a solution-oriented culture (which is certainly not a bad thing), but in the face of trauma and the loss of children, it's not as easy as waiting for tangible signs of goodness to reconcile all that has happened. Sometimes we're here in the wake of loss, just floating and breathing and wondering if we're doing it right. This is the part where we endure, and persevere, and press on. Nobody ever uses the words "press on" in pleasant life circumstances. The pressing on is for the times when all is not how we want it to be.

I honestly can remember the day I got so sick of hearing the word "endure." I guess I had been reading so many infant loss articles and blogs that the word became a frustrating concept that nagged at me from the back of my brain. Hearing it made me cringe, and I could never pinpoint why.

Now I realize it's because I am just plain old tired of enduring. That's sort of a weird concept, right? What does persevering even mean, and how do I have the ability to be tired of it? So one day, in my frustration, I looked up the definition of endure. It's almost humorous. We think sometimes that to endure means to stay strong and to pray and to put our best face forward as we trudge through the mess. But the definition is actually much more simple:

to suffer patiently, and
to tolerate.

That's it.

It may sound pitiful, but that definition brought me so much comfort. You could not have paid me enough money to muster up any amount of "strength" in this. People kept telling me I was strong, but I felt the opposite. What does it mean to be strong in the midst of loss and heartache? I mean, I didn't opt out of living, so there's that, but I wouldn't consider that fact to be a marker of personal strength and great endurance. What I could do is just be. I could tolerate. People would tell me I was strong and courageous for walking through this, and that they could never be strong enough to face such loss, but that never made sense to me. There wasn't a way I could snap my fingers and turn off the suffering or change the outcome. I was merely surrendering because I had no other choice. I didn't ask for this. I had no way out. We don't get to decide we aren't strong enough to handle something, and then have that situation not happen to us.

The pre-infant-loss version of myself could never have fathomed I would watch my children die. What that really means is that I didn't ever want to imagine a life with that as my reality. But now that I have experienced it, I know that we, as human beings, are capable of staring fear and loss and heartache and devastation in the face and not having it wreck us. Nobody welcomes hardship or pain to take over their lives. We live in a broken world where all is not as it should be. But what if we were more aware of how capable we are of walking through the valley and still being alive on the other side, to talk of our battle? I don't mean that we should invite danger and reckless behavior into our lives to test our ability to survive, but rather that we live bravely and boldly, unafraid of what lies ahead. Unafraid that our reality may look different than the one we grew up imagining. We are not promised a life void of pain, but what I do know from experience is that, if we let it, every unexpected trial can be used to tell the story of a life made stronger.

It was so hard to wake up each day and have all of this be the first thing that comes to mind. For a while, I was stuck on the topic of faith in the midst of all of this. Do we have faith that God can and does heal? Do we have faith that he's holding us through this? And every question that came to mind ended in a yes; we do have faith. We never lost sight of that. But there was something nagging at me that went so much deeper than the topic of faith, and it was a question I started asking myself every day: Am I physically and emotionally capable of getting through this? Is there really going to be life on the other side of losing our children to a disorder that appears to be without cause? Am I ever going to recover from this?

I found that in the midst of mourning my children, I mourned the loss of the care-free versions of ourselves. I missed the couple that stood at the front of our wedding, blissfully unaware of the life full of heartache and the robbed memories with our children into which we would enter. Sometimes people talk about how they wouldn't change their traumatic experience if they could because of how much it impacted their life for the good. To be completely real with you, there are some days I would agree with this. And there are other days where, if I were given the option to snap my fingers and have never experienced it, I would.

Maybe that's why many people who have found themselves in our shoes choose to terminate their pregnancies; so they can get it over with and move on. I totally get it. And we aren't condemning these people. We are making the point that we live in a society that doesn't want for anything. We live in a solution-oriented society where it is counter-cultural to endure. Why endure when you can find a solution? Just fix it, as best as you can, and move on. That tendency and way of thinking can be toxic when we're finally faced with circumstances that are so far beyond our understanding and our threshold for pain. The opposite of enduring in our case would have been to either control the situation by ending the life of this human growing in our womb, or for us to completely opt out of this life. And I genuinely do not believe that terminating Ellie's and Elsie's lives early would come without its own set of baggage, emotional hardship, and grief.

Snapping our fingers and having it all disappear wasn't an option. The only option for us was to endure by tolerating. I found that to be so liberating and so free of pressure. I didn't need to muster up the courage to "endure properly," whatever that means. I didn't need to put on a mask of fake inner strength and find reasons to tell people why it was all going to be okay. I just needed to allow time to pass and to continue to remember that infant loss, although it was now an irreplaceable part of my story, would not define me. The loss would only wreck me if I let it.

13

Finding Yourself

Our experience in not having Elsie here with us has been similar to what it was like after Ellie, but with an added layer of grief in that we ache for both of them at the same time. Considering Ellie and Elsie's pregnancies (and the gap between the two) was about two years of time, we've realized that half of our marriage and life together thus far has been incredibly intense! If I think about that for too long I start to realize that my outlook on life can be rather dark. A far cry from my pre-infant loss, joyfully optimistic self. With the introduction of death came the introduction of conflict and disunity in our family. We struggled to see eye-to-eye as we attempted to combat defeat in our hearts. We lost the ability to dream and to ponder the incredible experiences that might be ahead. We really lost our footing and found ourselves trying to dissect everything about life and our personalities and our marriage in order to pinpoint where things were out of sync and fix them and move on.

The problem was that this was the new normal, and we hadn't learned to cope with it yet. It felt as if we should be able to emotionally and mentally disassemble life as we knew it, and reassemble it in a way that made sense and move on from there. But it turns out that sitting in the discomfort and the pain would be the only way to realize that life was going to be different now, and that we weren't necessarily broken. We were just experiencing a new reality that we didn't ask for. It's so difficult to mourn your children, and what I've learned is that I now mourn the loss of who I used to be before walking through all of this. I'm not the same and I can't go back.

In fact, I frequently think about how different my worldview would be had I never experienced all of this, and sometimes I can begin to lose myself in wondering what happened to that happy-go-lucky version of my former self. This sort of grief becomes a part of you. It changes most things about you in ways that people who haven't experienced it can't understand. Outsiders looking in may wonder why it's taking us to long to get over this. I've heard that a lot from fellow infant loss parents. They will frequently express the frustration of family members or friends who can't seem to understand why we all can't just "move on", but even if I choose not to talk about my children, it doesn't mean I'm not always thinking of them. So I can either share my heart out loud or keep it in, but these are the things we are feeling. There's nothing wrong with us. Every good parent thinks about their children hundreds of times every single day. This doesn't change just because they aren't on earth.

I was talking with another mom who lost her children as well, and she said that grief is like something that we wear. It's not that grief takes a part of our former self away and replaces it with a gaping hole. It's that we have been thrust into a situation in which we have taken grief on, and we can learn to wear it well, or we can wear it in a way that disrupts us. That may seem morbid or sad, like imagining a little ball of grief forever sitting on one shoulder, always asking to be talked to and entertained. But really, it is an added layer of experience, made up of memories of our children who are supposed to be home in our arms. I would never wish the memory of them away, and so I learn to see the world through this new lens. It's not better and it's not worse. But it's different, and that's okay. We can't continue to put pressure on ourselves to be who we were before all this happened. We would never ask a soldier to forget that they went to war. This changes you, and there is something to be said about taking the time to rediscover yourself in new light.

I used to get down on myself for not being over-the-moon each time another friend or family member told us they were pregnant. It always seemed so easy for them, and as time passed, I would watch as new babies were added and added again to families with ease. I don't mean that having multiple babies is easy. I mean that pregnancies without complications, ultrasounds with happy endings, and car rides home with newborns seem so foreign to me that I couldn't believe it seemed to happen so regularly all around me. It can feel so lonely knowing that what happened to us is a rarity. I'm glad our experience isn't the norm, but it can be hard to relate when the world around you reflects something so opposite to your experience.

I finally got to the point mentally where I realized that happiness, well wishes, sadness, and an aching heart can exist in the same moment together. Why do we insist that we must feel each and every emotion full-on and fully independent of any other emotion? It seems so obviously flawed to think this way, and yet it feels much nicer to feel strong emotions exclusively. I genuinely felt excited for my friends and family, but also genuinely felt like punching through my walls and banging my head against my pillow. Freedom came when I realize that this is perfectly acceptable. I am owning the right to experience a whole lot of feelings in any given moment. Hopefully you have people around you who recognize this and encourage it. If not, journaling is probably a good idea. Or yelling at a tree. Or punching your pillow.

I was talking to our counselor recently about this, and he encouraged me to run away from the feelings if I want to. Not for forever. But if they are too overwhelming at any given point in time, I can go to one of my "happy places": the gym, the beach, or engaging in an activity that keeps my mind busy. At first I wanted to believe that this was the worst advice, because then I may never deal with my feelings. But, I do think that there are times to look into the face of grief and mourning, and times to give your mind a rest. On the flip side, I was told also to sit in the feelings at times, even if it means heavy tears and angry fits of throwing air punches. I have learned so much about my threshold for emotional pain through the process of grieving. I know my limits and I know when to push myself. This can be such a valuable gift after loss.

Speaking of knowing our limits, I never realized before I lost my girls how many movies and television shows depict the loss of children. I don't think I noticed it before. This can be a *huge trigger*, especially when the scenes pop up unexpectedly. I actively avoid movies and shows with plots revolving around the loss of children as I have learned that I simply can't handle it. Even shows with a lot of birthing scenes can be awful for me personally. These are things we learn as we walk forward. We learn our new limits and boundaries through trial and error and it's all a part of discovering how to take care of ourselves and keep ourselves healthy. I have so many friends and family members who warn me about certain television shows, movies, even blog posts or news articles floating around that might send us into a bad place. Talk to your friends. Let them know how you're feeling so that they can take care of you in that way.

14

Comfort in Mourning

I can't even begin to imagine what it was like for our friends and family to walk through this again with us. That may seem silly since we were the ones actually going through it. But I would be remiss if I didn't acknowledge what a challenge it must have been for them to know what to say, what to do, and how to act around us. Not to mention, most of my closest friends were also pregnant and due within four or five months of Elsie's due date.

Many of them have told me that they have not been strangers to survivor's guilt. I can absolutely understand that. One of the hardest parts about grieving within community was that I had to be brutally honest about what helped and what didn't help. It may sound harsh or insensitive for us to be picky about how others help us, but there's a reason why we think it's important.

Grieving the death of a child is certainly not easy, and receiving comfort can be tricky. It's hard to know what comments, kind gestures, and encounters are going to trigger pain. It can add a layer of extreme discomfort to the already difficult process of grieving. Maybe you've seen articles and blog posts with titles like, "What Not to Say to an Infant-Loss Mom, etc." Those articles must be challenging to read for someone who hasn't experienced loss or doesn't know anyone who has experienced it. But I do think it's important that honesty remains the priority in helping others help you. Yes, they can bring discomfort as onlookers read on the edge of their seats, not knowing if they will subsequently regret something they've said. But, I believe there is value in transparency, especially in light of grief.

I remember discovering that flowers were a huge emotional trigger for me. Doesn't that sound so weird? I would see them all over our apartment in vases of all kinds, and all I could think about when I saw them was that they were slowly dying before my eyes. This might sound crazy to some. But before losing children, that thought never crossed my mind when looking at a beautiful bouquet of flowers. Loss like this can change everything about how you view the world. I began to realize that while it might be uncomfortable to tell people not to send flowers, it would be easier for them to handle this seemingly awkward request than it would be for me to continue staring at dying flowers in those early days and weeks of waking up without my babies at home. Those first days and weeks following loss are especially raw. You see everything through the filter of your loss, even flowers. It may seem trivial or overly-sensitive to onlookers, but the reality is that everything about coming home without a child you've birthed is confusing and disorienting. Things that used to bring you joy and comfort now remind you of the sting of death.

I talked to other grieving mothers who loved receiving flowers because it reminded them of the life that still existed all around them, as well as others who felt the exact same way I did. There's really no way to know any of this until you are walking through it.

Between frequent visits with friends and acquaintances, there were days when I would wake up feeling relatively normal, and then we would get a knock at the door of a friend with a warm meal. My heart would skip a beat as I remembered that we were being brought food because our child was dead. It was as if my mind was so determined to block out the pain that, when I wasn't talking to somebody about what we were going through, it could seem, even briefly, like things were normal. I don't necessarily think this is a healthy thing, but it is often the default state of my brain in the midst of emotional pain.

Receiving meals even just a few weeks without Elsie was a jarring reminder that we were in a really tough spot. That can seem self-centered and ungrateful given the act of sweet friends bringing us food, but there was never a time where I was angry about it. I just felt so desperate for normalcy. That said, I am ever grateful for every single person who stepped into our world to comfort us in any way they chose to do so. Truthfully.

The second I returned home from the hospital after Ellie, empty-armed and heartbroken, I went straight to the washer and dryer to start a load of laundry. My body was tired and sore from delivering Ellie, but I was determined to get back to some sort of routine. I didn't want to be fussed over or made to sit down because sitting down and being served gave me all of the time in the world to think about what had happened. I knew that, deep down, I couldn't pretend nothing had happened and get back to the way things used to be. But I think that there are times in the process of grief where our brains just say no. I felt like I needed just a few moments to do my laundry myself, or make a meal myself, or load the dishwasher to feel some sort of connection to the mundane, rather than a connection to the extreme situation of being cared for because my child was gone.

I know that there are plenty of hurting people out

there who are happy to receive meals for extended periods of time; this certainly proves that everyone grieves differently and that there isn't a one size fits all for how comfort should happen. The best thing I felt I could do was write publicly about what we were experiencing as positively as possible. I never wanted friends and family to feel nervous about attempting to help us in our grief, but I knew that I didn't have the ability to cope as well with all of these little things as I would have in everyday life outside of all of the chaos.

The worst situation you can find yourself in is when you, the grieving individual, are faced with the task of "caring for others" in conversation with them. You will start to feel like you're filtering your true thoughts and feelings in order to make sure you don't make the person on the other end of the conversation feel uncomfortable. I knew I didn't want to pretend like everything was great and helpful, fearful that my suppressed emotions would one day explode. Those first few days and weeks after loss can feel so fragile that the slightest amount of stress will push you over the edge. Your job in those fresh, raw moments of loss is not to take care of those around you. It is to allow yourself to be cared for.

What did help was sharing wine with friends who expected honest answers from us when they ask us how we are doing, and who made us laugh often. We tried hard to only surround ourselves with people who were uplifting and life-giving and who encouraged us to be free in what we were feeling at all times. If we needed to cry we could, and if we were feeling joyful we knew we didn't need to feel guilty about it. I found that I needed my "safe" people to text and call at any moment with whatever I was feeling Their ability to be those safe people for us is not lost on me. I found that all of my "safe" people could be described very similarly: they were all transparent, easy-going, and able to put themselves in our shoes. They frequently asked open-ended questions like, "Is it helpful when [situation], " or "How does it make you feel when [this] happens?" They never tried to solve our issues of grief, as doing so would be impossible. They simply tried to be there, in it, with us.

They knew that nothing they said would take away the pain, but they were willing to walk side by side with us. If they asked us how we were doing and we responded with a simple "fine," they would probe further, not out of disbelief, but out of a commitment to make sure we were being taken care of. They would ask us if we wanted to talk about Ellie and Elsie, or if we would rather not. They spoke of Ellie and Elsie like they were real people and never tried to act like they never happened. They never spoke to us as if we weren't parents.

That has been one of the hardest parts for me in

grieving. I don't have other children at home, yet I have all of the feelings that only a mother can feel. The maternal part of my heart has been turned on, and I can't express those nurturing feelings and qualities towards my own children because they aren't here. The strong, loving feelings that a parent feels towards their child does not turn off when away from their presence. It hurts deeply to have such strong feelings of love and bonding towards two small people who we know we will never get to see again on this earth. Once you have (or adopt) children, you are inherently a parent, and being treated as if you've never had children hurts my heart worse than most things.

Sure, we can't weigh in on many conversations about the practical ins-and-outs of raising our children, but our hearts and minds don't just return back to the way they were before we were pregnant. I remember talking with someone a couple months after the birth and death of Elsie who was acknowledging characteristics of my husband that were going to be really awesome *once we had children*, and all I could think about was how I knew he was a good father long ago when I watched him carry our daughter's coffin and lower it into the ground. I knew he was a good father every single time he placed his head next to my belly and spoke to his daughters with love and laughter. I subsequently thought about how I watched him sleep in the hospital room with our second deceased daughter on his chest and wondered, with a broken heart, how I got so lucky to have such a strong, yet tender man to father our children.

People don't have memories of those moments like I do. I try to practice a lot of grace when those kinds of conversations happen, knowing their intent is not to harm, but it can be very challenging. My heart aches deeply when I think about the army of childless parents out there, aching for their children with a parental bond that never can be satisfied. We've also had people learn of our story and then tell us, "Well, I suppose it's just not your time to be parents." I doubt I even need to address the various insensitive and incorrect facets of this statement, but it is a good example of the kinds of things people will say out of ignorance. I don't believe that children die because their parents aren't meant to be parents. The thought of that is cruel and absurd. Children die because our world is broken and not as it should be. It is impossible to read Scripture and not come to grips with this truth.

My best advice for grieving parents, or grieving individuals in general, is to be honest about what you need. It's also a good idea not to resort to violence when it comes to the crazy things people say. I'm kidding of course, but am I actually kidding? I could write an entire book about the crazy things people said to us, and still say to us, through it all. Be honest about what helps, and be honest about what doesn't. Although people don't always know the best ways to help, if they genuinely do want to help, they will receive what you have to say with an open heart. My best advice for those helping their grieving friend or family member is to ask them questions and expect honest answers. Try your hardest not to have an offendable heart, so that you can aid them in the most effective way possible. We should extend grace to one another in all situations and matters of life, but we should especially extend grace to those who are deeply hurting. I have said my fair share of things that never would have come to my mind or mouth had I not been in a place of despair.

15

When the World Continues to Turn

After both Ellie and Elsie, I experienced a similar feeling at months three and four post-delivery. Three or four months seems to be about the amount of time it takes for people to start checking in less with you, and I don't mean that in a judgmental way. Life does go on and I never expected anyone to call, text, write letters, and visit as much as they did previously, but this is the time when the grief can hit hard. I was seeing more babies born, more friends announce their pregnancies, as well as seeing the seasons change and normal life pick back up again. For me, I was still stuck in a place of very real grief, mourning, and general sadness that my girls weren't here with me. I felt, both times, like the world around me was already forgetting what we had been through, although I know that this is not the truth.

I felt jealous that people were moving on and able

to experience the normal joys of life. I didn't wish grief or despair onto them, as I knew that I couldn't expect it to stay so fresh (nor did I want it to) for everyone around us. *But the level of grief I felt at month three and four post-death was not that much different than it was the day they passed away.* I was no longer at home crying all day, but the ache in my heart was equally as shocking and equally as deep when each of them left the earth. Even the most mundane of daily activities, such as grocery shopping or going to the gym, could pose a giant challenge. Imagine walking past the baby aisle of every grocery store. You may not notice how many baby products are advertised all around you, but let me just tell you that the baby products are not contained solely in the baby aisle. The posters and coupons and displays stick out like a billboard in front of your face.

I can't tell you how many times I cried at the gym as I attempted to get back into shape. Your body feels so different after giving birth. These differences are a physical reminder that your body once held a life that no longer exists. Don't even get me started about seeing pregnant women at the gym, or anywhere for that matter. I distinctly remember multiple times where I had to quit my workout and go home because of the progression of thoughts I would think. Imagine stepping onto a treadmill after that first six weeks of postpartum recovery. Your body feels different. As you begin to workout, your mind is consumed with the status of the new shape of your maternal figure. I would begin to workout and then feel crippled by the thought that I was working off my baby body with no baby to show for it when I was done. I didn't get to step off the treadmill and go home to my little ones. I was attempting to get my body back without the reward of seeing their faces and knowing it was all worth it. I cannot change clothes or shower without seeing my cesarean section scar. I can't change clothes or shower without seeing my stretch marks. But the precious lives who gave them to me aren't around.

This grief felt much more lonely than the grief I had previously been experiencing, and it became harder for me to reach out to friends and family about what I was feeling because I would feel guilty for bringing up our situation once again. I continuously felt like bringing up my pain would bring others down. Then, I would feel even worse for bringing sadness to the seemingly happy lives of those around me. I also didn't like feeling like people would perceive me as being needy or dramatic. I realize this sounds ridiculous as I type it, but grief is so complicated--it's hard to think clearly sometimes! I occasionally forced myself to reach out to a friend and simply say, "Please pray," but I wish I had been more vocal about my grief in those months. I just hated to feel like I was being a burden.

This was also about the time that I started to feel guilty about the thoughts I had towards other babies that were making their appearance, either in the womb or entering into the world after birth. Feelings of envy and anger and guilt surfaced frequently as I thought, "Seriously? Another healthy baby with no complications!? How is this possible!" I mentioned this before, but because my whole world of pregnancy and parenthood has been filled with nothing but tragedy, sickness, and death, it began to feel like these things were the norm. But they simply are not. Those who lose children are in the minority, and while I'm thankful that that's the truth, it sets the stage for a tough life when it comes to the multiple bundles of joy that seem to come with ease all around you. I never wanted to see any baby around me struggle or die so that I would feel less alone, but I did struggle with a lot of "why me" moments as babies came to families close to me with such ease.

Occasionally, I battled guilt for wondering why all the babies around me were so healthy. I would find myself almost surprised to hear about another uncomplicated twenty-week anatomy scan. I thought that surely I couldn't be the only one in my circles of family and friends who had to deal with something like this. You know those advertisements that use the graphic for statistics where one figure out of a sea of many is highlighted a different color to point out the frequency in which some sort of phenomenon occurs? Like, "Did you know that one out of every

[however many] people deals with [such and such]?"
Each time a new person in my life found out their
pregnancy was going well or their baby was birthed
and didn't die, I would see myself as that highlighted
person. I was the statistic. I was the one who won
the most awful lottery of all--twice. Alone in a sea of
normal pregnancies and normal births, waving my
hands in the crowd as I attempted to find another
who could understand what I was experiencing.
Luckily, and also sadly, I was not alone. I found it
super helpful to get connected with a couple of infant-
loss groups on social media, although I didn't always
have the strength to check in often with them. I took
great comfort in the fact that there were others out
there who knew what I was feeling. Even if I couldn't
identify with everything they were experiencing and
how they were grieving, it helped me to feel not so
alone. I keep in touch with a few of the people I've
met who have experienced the loss of a child, and we
compare notes often on how we're holding up and
what has been helping us along. The situations don't
always look the same as mine (in fact, I've only met
one other person who has lost two children back-to-
back with no other children at home) but it's helpful
nonetheless to explore my feelings in a place where
people understand from experience.

16

Loss and Infertility

I can't claim to know what traditional infertility looks like, but I am walking through a sort of infertility as we are unable to carry healthy biological children of our own. Or, at least that's the conclusion we must come to after inconclusive genetic testing. It is quite frustrating to me that on top of the fatal diagnoses themselves, I am faced with the fact that Chris could look at me the wrong way and I'd get pregnant. To be highly fertile, only to create children who cannot live outside the womb is quite the dilemma. Finding this out added a different layer of grief when walking through it with Elsie, as I had no idea that I'd experience it all over again after Ellie died.

We previously thought, due to the theories of the doctors, that what happened with Ellie was an anomaly, and so the loss of biological motherhood was not on my radar. This time I had to come face-to-face with dealing with permanent birth control solutions at age twenty-five, which is not something of which I could have perceived I would deal. From a young age, having biological children was my biggest dream and desire. Dealing with this part of things has been made easier by entering into the world of adoption (which is something we wanted to do regardless of what we've been through with our biological children), but I can't pretend like it heals the wound entirely. I have mourned the loss of biological motherhood just as I have mourned my children, and seeing pregnant women out and about still touches that wound on my heart. I don't know for certain that it will get easier as the years go by. But I am hopeful that I am able to cope better and better as time goes on.

It's such a challenge to deal with infertility in a world where child abuse and unwanted pregnancies riddle the news channels daily. It sheds new light on the issue of abortion and embryo destruction in lab settings, and it angers me deeply and on a completely new level to hear of the latest mother on the news who has murdered her children. There is this deep longing for justice and mercy, and sometimes, it's too intense for me to handle. I don't really have any ground-breaking thoughts about how to deal with this stuff other than to say that it completely sucks. It's not even okay. It is unfair and it is not easy and excuse me while I punch the wall again.

This is a hurdle that I have to jump over time and time again in my faith. Why did God put this deep desire in me to have biological children? I know plenty of people who could go either way when it comes to having children or not having children, and yet I'm here with this deep desire that ended tragically twice in a row. It's hard to come to grips with this as I pray about it. But, I have realized often through scripture that God has revealed His heart in the matter. Pause and read Isaiah 65.

I can't pretend that reading Scripture brings me to a place of peace about every time, but it does remind me that there is something larger going on here, and that things won't always be this way. If I profess to believe that God's Word is true, then I am accepting with open arms the truth that redemption is going to happen once and for all.

Knowing this truth doesn't always make living in the here-and-now easier. This promise does bring comfort to my heart, but dealing with infertility and loss in a practical sense is complicated and messy. During both of my pregnancies, there were a combined total of eleven babies born in close social circles, three of which were my immediate family. My nephew, who I adore, was born during Elsie's funeral.

I can't explain what it felt like to see healthy delivery after healthy delivery. I couldn't log onto the computer without seeing news of a new baby every

month or so. Sometimes, multiple babies came within
weeks of each other. I certainly hoped none of them
would face complications, but the continual stream of
health and new life felt so isolating. I was continually
reminded of what pregnancy and delivery is supposed
to look like. I was continually reminded that I would
likely never experience that joy.

Although seeing each new child enter the world
was confusing and conflicting, I am blessed to say
that my friends and family were consistently sensitive
and compassionate towards me.

One family in particular, The Sanders, were
pregnant with their fourth boy during my pregnancy
with Elsie. I will never forget the day Megan called
me to tell me what they wanted to name him. She
asked if I would be okay if they made his middle
name Jordan. His name would be Solace Jordan.
They both loved the name Jordan and felt it would
be fitting for him. She went on to explain that they
also wanted to honor our family and that she never
wanted to forget, in the chaos and challenge of raising
multiple children, that life could be so different. She
always wanted to remember our girls. I cried as she
told me this. I felt so cared for. I knew that all of my
pregnant friends and family were in a rough spot.
They were walking alongside me in my grief, all the
while knowing I wouldn't experience their joy as they
welcomed their new children into the world. The

honor and power behind his name would soon mean
even more to me.

At just a few months old, he would already be
living up to his name. There were times after Elsie
left that I teetered on the edge of losing my will to
live. I wasn't suicidal by any means, but there were
many moments where I could clearly see how the loss
we faced could wreck me and the rest of my life. I
could see clearly how the resentment and bitterness
and anger and sorrow could begin to spiral into a life
of darkness.

It was as if the path of the rest of my life was laid
before me, splitting into two directions. One direction
would take endurance, grace, pruning, and healing,
but it would lead to great hope. The other merely
required that I put one foot in front of the other and
survive each day. It would lead to bitterness and a life
unfulfilled and void of true purpose. It was during
those moments that the Lord would bring Solace to
mind. I would remember his middle name, and the
courage to choose life would return to my heart. I
needed to leave a legacy of bravery and endurance.
I didn't want him to know his name was associated
with someone who gave it all up, overcome by pain.

The Lord was giving me tangible reminders that I
needed to choose which path to take. This particular
reminder came in the form of a healthy baby boy.
He was nudging me to choose hope and joy rather

than mere survival. I believe that, when we surround ourselves with friends who are close to God, they will be used to speak life into our spirits. This is absolutely necessary in our walk through the valley.

17

Learning to Hope

When I was studying psychology in college, we had to learn the popular theory of the "Five Stages of Grief". I learned it, was tested on it, and made sense of the theory, but now I remember that theory and admittedly scoff at how simple it describes the process of mourning. The five stages of grief, if you haven't heard them, are: denial, anger, bargaining, depression, and acceptance. This theory of grief was first proposed by Elisabeth Kubler-Ross in her book, "On Death and Dying." The reason for my previously sassy attitude towards this theory was solely based on the fact that it seemed so clinical and detached. It writes as if we move steadily between one "phase" to the next until arriving at the final, sobering phase of acceptance.

For example, it's easy to read about depression when you're not depressed, and to skim over the complicated beast that it is. In fact, I *do* remember studying it in a purely objective sense with no personal connection to it. The problem is that it's not just a stage of grief; it's a monster of an experience that can last any number of months or years if left to its own devices. But Kubler-Ross' work is a prime example of how grief is an experience that can't be adequately explained with words or scientific studies. It's an individualized experience with a wide variety of layers, and I admire her for putting a name to the face of all of those insane and ever-changing feelings.

I bring up her work because of hope. Hope in the face of denial looks different than hope in the face of anger. And hope certainly looks different in the face of bargaining, especially bargaining for the life of a loved one, than it does in the face of depression. I experienced great hope, albeit hope mixed with tons of anger, during my pregnancy with Elsie, because of the fact that she was still alive and still with me and there was still time left to pray. My hope for her was dependent on, and intertwined with, what was happening in her life. As long as she was alive in the womb, I felt that I had great hope for her life. In reality, I think that I was dealing with a bit of denial regarding our circumstances. I think that's okay. I desperately needed to find ways to cope with another half-year of intense stress, and so I don't regret for one minute the hope for a positive prognosis for my daughter.

I realized that acceptance in grieving doesn't have to be a one-time thing. In light of the stages of grief, I thought that I would maybe wake up one day and experience this great revelation of acceptance and subsequently feel some sort of intense peace about moving forward. Instead, there are days when I wake up back in denial that my girls aren't going to be here for the long haul. Other days, I find that I can accept that they won't be here with us in this lifetime, and the realization is not paralyzing. I don't think there is any rhyme or rhythm to this wavering acceptance, but I do believe it will get easier with time.

Now I realize why the topic of hope is so emphasized in the Bible. Outside of all circumstances that we can see is a hope that exists solely because of what God has done. I knew deep down that, if Ellie and Elsie lived, it would be a victory, and that if they died it would also be a victory, but I saw the hope related to them dying as less of a victory than their healthy lives here on this earth. It's just so hard to have hope regarding what we cannot see. But hope in the work that Jesus did on the cross is a hope that cannot be underemphasized. It certainly doesn't take away the pain here and now, but it is so worth treasuring in my heart.

18

An Interview With My Husband

It is my understanding that men often get left out of the conversation about pregnancy, infertility, and infant loss. I remember reading one article about loss that pinpointed "infant-loss mothers," in the title, and then getting to the end and seeing a few comments from infant-loss fathers who felt isolated and disregarded. I totally agreed. Men who experience loss may not be as vocal about their experiences (or maybe some are!), but that doesn't make their feelings or thoughts about it less valuable. Women process loss so differently than men, and I want to honor my husband and all the other men who are fathers of babies in Heaven. The following questions were answered by my sweet husband, one year after our second loss.

What was it like for you to find out your unborn baby would not survive past birth?

Finding out about Ellie was so crazy from the start, because I was in nursing school and we didn't necessarily plan for her. The thought of being a parent was exciting and scary at the same time. So going into it feeling all these different emotions, and then going to the twenty-week ultrasound was shocking. I never considered what happened an option that would be in front of us. At first, I thought it was an error. I thought we would find out the technician was wrong. Week after week, appointment after appointment- it was the same bad news over and over.

Finding out about Elsie was, once again, similar to how I felt about Ellie. We were told it wouldn't happen again, so the year of emotional recovery where we processed what happened with Ellie allowed me to get to a place where I was ready. The doctors were so confident that I didn't expect to hear that news again. I had just gotten to the place where I felt ready to be a parent again. With Ellie, there was so much distraction for me because of school. I didn't get to pour a lot of my energy and time into thinking about her the way I did with Elsie. In one sense, it was better with Elsie during the pregnancy for me, because I could be more present and build a deeper relationship with her. That twenty-week ultrasound with her was so unexpected, and hearing those words was almost surreal. It didn't feel like it was actually happening. We were so excited and we had so much hope and it was like we were taken to a deeper, lower level than ever before.

How did you cope with the impending loss?

Coping was a lot different each time. With Ellie, my natural coping mechanism was to block it out. I tried not to think about it too much. I prayed, but my prayer was very limited. I almost pretended it wasn't happening. It was debilitating to think of it a lot...but because I'm a guy and because I wasn't carrying her physically, I was able to shut that part of my brain down. The times I did think about it, I would get so upset and so sick to my stomach that I couldn't do anything at all. I knew I needed to get through nursing school. That made me feel like I wasn't strong and that I wasn't helping Jordan. That made me want to ignore the whole situation even more. I don't like the way I dealt with it all, but in the midst of it I didn't know any other way.

But for Elsie, it was a much different experience. Our pastor in Charleston and our close community were very influential in allowing us to pursue God's Kingdom and His heart for the situation. For one, I asked Him to be there and I asked him to save her life. The experience with Elsie was so much better, as horrible as it was. The time I had with her was amazing, and I felt like I could get to know her, even in Jordan's womb.

What was most helpful to you during the hardest moments?

The thing that is most helpful to me is to remember the moments we had with the girls. It's very painful to do, but looking at pictures of Ellie and Elsie and then being filled with hope that we will see them again always help me most in the hard moments.

What was it like meeting your babies?

It was amazing meeting them...of course it wasn't amazing for them to leave, but it was a blur of emotions. It was so happy and sad at the same time. I loved getting to meet them. I felt connected to them, but it was also so hard. I didn't ever want to let them go. It was so painful because, in our joy, I knew they weren't going to continue on with us.

How do you process the whole experience differently than your wife?

I think the biggest difference is that everything Jordan experiences is happening together and in a connected way. I have the ability to, in a way, put everything in a compartment and not think about it for a while. That can lead to a lot of confusing emotions, though. The tendency is for me to want to ignore [it] rather than face it. Jordan's natural tendency is to write or reach out to friends, but when I reach out, I tend to ask for practical advice. It's not necessarily helpful for me to sit down and explore my feelings, but rather I look at what's happening in my life and what actions I can take to get through it. This doesn't mean I'm not feeling, it just means I'm handling my feelings in a different way. It took Jordan time to realize that my logical way of dealing with my pain wasn't easier, it was just different.

What advice do you have for men walking through loss with their wives?

The number one thing I would suggest is to carve out as much time as you can with God. Things would have been different with Ellie if I had been closer to God. Making that a priority, and being as open as you can with your spouse makes all the difference. Try to find a spiritual leader you can be open and transparent with. It is hard no matter how strong you are, and it helps to talk to males who are comfortable with being vulnerable to help you process what's going on. It's so hard to process by yourself. When you're going through it, there are so many emotions... and we can tend to bottle it up and compartmentalize it.

How did infant loss change your perspective on life?

Infant loss shook up my worldview, especially related to how God interacts with us. In a way, I discovered a part of God that was more emotional. It felt like He was close to us and that He knew the pain we were feeling. I can trust God easier now because I know that he is for our family and that he wants good things for us. The way it's changed my perspective is that anything can happen to you. Sometimes we get so consumed with the idea of safety that we take for granted the life we have and how many variables there are that can change instantly. We can't ever be prepared for how things can change, but you can't allow this to induce fear. That's why it's so important for me to have a hopeful view of life. When you hold to hope, the worry and the what-ifs fall away.

How did infant loss impact your marriage?

nervous laughter Well, for a while there it was super rough. I think the hardest thing was that I felt like, for the first time in our marriage, we were on different pages. When we were dating and the first bit of marriage before Ellie, we were so unified and it was so comforting. I was so confident in our relationship. It was strong... and so, for the first time, things got frustrating. I came to a point where I didn't know how to fix things, and that's always my natural instinct. I knew I couldn't fix the situation and I could only be there for Jordan, knowing it wouldn't make things easier or less painful. As the leader [of our marriage], I was trying to be sensible and logical and the anchor for our family. I didn't want to let our emotions derail us. It's been one of the most challenging things, but I am so grateful for our commitment to one another. It's given me confidence to be able to move forward and truly be able to say we are for each other and we are in this together.

19

Not Having It Together

I mentioned that I write in a family blog about my life and have done so since 2009. This can be a tricky thing when it comes to processing feelings, because a lot of times I can reach the end of a blog post and feel the need to neatly package my thoughts with a nice, clean conclusion or resolution. I believe that, for the most part, people understand that my journal is just a snippet into my thought-life. But, occasionally people will misinterpret each ending to signify that I am through dealing with any given issue. I wanted to be careful in ending this book in not giving off the impression that I am a "professional griever" or someone who has got it all together. I didn't want to offer solutions to every facet of infant loss, because I spend most of my days fumbling around this life that still appears to be mine. I definitely don't have the solutions, even if I wanted to claim that I do.

Handling all of this often feels more like being dragged around by it, and then attempting to find your footing every now and again. I don't remember ever making any coherent decisions about how I am going to make it through all of this. Rather, I find myself stumbling upon what helps and what doesn't help and allowing that help to be my guide. I can simply choose, continually, to seek righteousness rather than degradation. I want people to be aware of how many times I tell myself to just keep breathing.

Maybe there are other infant loss parents out there who really are doing okay. I wish nothing more than for this to be true for everyone who walks this road. At the same time, it's important to know that it's okay to not feel okay, and to not feel strong, and to not feel like you're handling all of this in the best way. There is no best way to walk through this. There are certainly healthy ways and unhealthy ways to cope, but my point is that you don't need to feel the pressure to seem strong or save face with people. You're allowed to feel what you're feeling and to navigate this in a million different ways.

One thing I know to be true is that this is not the end, and that the loss of my children does not define who I am unless I let it. Instead, you can reap blessing from loss, as you have the powerful ability to empathize with those who have walked the same road. Your words. Your embrace. Your prayers.

Everything you have to offer is from the first hand experience of deep pain and sorrow and the hope that can follow. You have the ability to tell a story full of redemption, even if you never see that redemption with your physical eyes. I don't know if it's because of the movies and television shows we grow up watching, but I never realized until recently how much I subconsciously believed that, when things are really bad, they can't possibly get worse. We are constantly exposed to fictional stories of tragedy that suddenly turn around for the better. It is not often that we hear of tragedy met with more tragedy.

Those types of stories are reserved for the news. That's probably why I don't watch the news. I now realize that redemption and joy and victory are guaranteed to me in Heaven. They are guaranteed to me because I know the saving power of Jesus. But while we're here, our jobs are not to chase happiness or control. They are not to choose what we perceive to be the easy way out. Our jobs are to love well and to live courageously until the time that all of it will be made right.

I have asked two of my best friends to contribute to this book because one perspective that I lack is that of a friend who chooses to walk through the valley with you. It takes true friendship to weather the intensity of loss, especially as they navigate how to love and support while being pregnant and while bringing healthy children into the world as you experience loss and grief. You'll hear from my best friends, Megan and Sarah, who remain my truest friends to this day.

> *To the brave one walking with the beautiful and broken, from Sarah*

I am a wife and mother of three beautiful, ginger haired children. My husband and I have one brilliantly wild daughter and two handsome boys who are the joy of our lives. My boys were supposed to have two lovely dark haired friends named Ellie and Elsie to grow up with, and I had the joy and also the sorrowful weight of being pregnant with my boys at the exact same time Jordan was pregnant with her girls.

We were the first people they told when they found out they were pregnant with Ellie, and we scooted right over to their little newlywed apartment to celebrate and reassure them that parenthood was amazing! And challenging! And beautiful! All the things! We had just found out that I was pregnant with our second child, and it was delightful to no end to dream with Jordan about our sweet babies growing up together. I have so often wished we all could have stayed in that space of suspended joy and naiveté. Infant loss, genetic abnormalities, newborn sized coffins: none of them were on our radar. We were all just full of dreams, delight, and new beginnings with our precious friends.

Weeks later, everything changed for the Tates when they found out Ellie would most likely not live outside the womb. The thing that should never be wished on anyone was happening to them and little did we know that when it was all said and done, that we would be witness to both of their girls passing into eternity at birth. Everything changed for all of us in their community in that space in time. How do you comfort your beloveds in that moment and the myriad moments after? Think about it: are there actual human words or sentiments that can make a mother or father's empty arms and broken heart feel normal, natural, or okay? Is there a meal train that I can arrange that will make them wake up one day and say, "Gosh! I feel like my old self!" It was staggering to begin to think of how to love and comfort them through this, because who has satisfactory answers for this sort of multiplied sorrow. It should have been a beautiful and amazing time for our families and community celebrating new life and babies. However, only our dreams came true. My first son was born healthy and thriving two months before Ellie, and my second son was born just one month from the day Elsie was born. The feeling of injustice that statement gives me takes my breath away every time.

The joy and honor of being present at Ellie's birth fell upon me. I was a part of helping give her the only bath she would ever receive, dress her in her only little dress and bonnet, and take her only pictures of her precious little earth side life. I will never forget her newborn baby smell, her sweet and crooked feet that were just so perfect, her curly black Tate hair. Watching my brave friends loving on her in their first moments as mama and daddy, oh, I remember every detail in painful and sacred clarity. They were brave and broken and beautiful all at once, and I felt on that day that all of Heaven was standing in honor of their choice to declare to the world that Ellie's life was of immeasurable value. Chris talked to Ellie like a proud daddy would, calling her all the sweet names in the book. Jordan watched them from her hospital bed with that look of mothering pride, watching the two people that made up her world together. It broke me in half in the best of ways.

If I could give the world a gift, it would be to know the thing I learned in that ugly, cold hospital room where glory and tragedy met. That there is no measure for the depth of the bottomless river of love that Father God holds for every soul He creates. That baby that they were told would be better off being terminated, that baby captured their hearts completely and it was obvious to everyone. And I got to witness it firsthand, up close and in my weeping, red face. I will never be the same. And I had no answers for them. Only tears and questions of my own.

I had no answers or words a week later when we gathered for her celebration of life and burial. My husband and a dear friend crafted her tiny casket of beautiful cherry wood. Our friend, Kim, sewed the lining for the box where her body would lay and made a small quilt and pillow to match. I was commissioned to paint the top of it with her name, birthdate, and some flowers. Everyone wore bright, happy colors at Jordan's request. I remember my friend Megan telling me through tears how she wanted to look pretty for Ellie. That day, Chris carried her little body in that box into the white chapel where my husband conducted the service. It was my husband Bryan's first funeral that he had ever attended. He wept at points as he bravely spoke of the life and hope of Christ, of how Ellie was whole and new and joyful beyond compare as she was made perfect in the presence of Jesus. Some sweet friends led us in song and Chris and Jordan just raised their hands in worship nearly the entire time. My husband and I served communion. I cried in a very undignified manner and could not have cared less. At the end, Chris took her little casket and carried her outside with Jordan at his side. It is a thing a father should never have to do, a mother the same. She was buried under three beautiful dogwood trees and then we all went home. Well, actually we all went to a bar and drank and cried and then went home. The next day, we woke up to the smiling faces of our two sweet children. They were too young to understand what had just happened. Our life went on, our children laughed, we made coffee, rocked on our porch, and watching our little ones play.

What do you say or do for someone when at the height of your personal joy, they are experiencing the unspeakable depths of soul crushing sorrow? Instead of loading a pink little bundle into a car seat for the first time, my friends loaded their baby girl's body into a tiny little box and laid her in the Earth. It was, and still is, something that I don't have adequate words for. How do you move forward in love, mercy, and grace, as you ignore the fear of screwing it up by saying or doing the wrong thing? There are so many opportunities to offer some awful platitude that would ring bitterly in their ears for years to come. My greatest fear was of saying something inadvertently cutting to them. I have seen the depth of their pain close up and the list thing I wanted was to add to it.

My only words of advice, if you could even call it that, or this: First, that fear you have that you will say or do something wrong as you're desperately trying to love and comfort the hurting ones in your life? Look it square in the eye and say, "I am not going to do this perfectly. I am going to do it anyway." Then just let your heart run at your people in their sorrow with all the love you can give. I know I have messed up when it has come to being a friend and a comforting presence to the Tate family and others in my life as they are experiencing sorrow. Do you know what I did when that happened? I apologized and asked for forgiveness and decided that I would not be afraid to try again.

There is so much grace to be experienced in walking through tragedy with loved ones. If we had decided to pull away from the Tates or them from us because it was too painful, we would have missed out on all the rejoicing! So, my last bit of advice? I am no expert by any means. Truly, there is only one expert when it comes to grief. Allow me to preach to myself and let you listen. Be humble and go straight to Jesus. You have nothing to give outside of Him but a few lame freezer meals and tepid condolences. Tell Him how you want to love the grieving as He does, but you don't know how. Tell Him what survivor's guilt feels like. Tell him how you don't know when to celebrate or cry. Let Him know that every time you have a friend go to an ultrasound these days, you pray so hard for a good outcome because you remember the times your friend's world came crashing down in those dark little rooms with sonogram machines. Ask Him the questions that you are pretty certain have no answer. Tell Him how it feels when joy is so often tinged with sorrow. Speak your words with insecurity and fear and fatigue right into His willing ears. And then listen to Him say what He says every time," I know. I know precious friend. I've been praying with you and for you as I always do. I understand. I hurt with them, I hurt with you. Now, let's go love together. Me flowing through you. Me meeting them sovereignly in ways you never will be able to. Let me be Me. Don't be afraid to be you and never be afraid to give love."

Go love, friends. Imperfectly and passionately. Embrace them in their grief and dance with them in their triumph. It's simple and painful and worth every tear shed or wiped from their faces.

The Richness of Suffering, from Megan

When we first heard Jordan and Chris were expecting we were so happy for them. At the time we had three boys of our own and were thrilled to share parenthood with our young friends. Then the worst news came and we learned of Ellie's issues. We did the only thing we knew to do: we prayed, and then we prayed some more. We called special prayer meetings and laid our hands on Jordan's beautiful, round belly, declaring life and not death. But, as you know, death did come and our hearts broke. I will never forget getting word Jordan was in labor. We were at the beach on vacation and my husband was the sickest I had ever seen him. I lay awake all night praying, battling what felt like Hell itself. I would intercede for the Tates and then for my husband, and then again for the Tates. I will never forget crying for an hour on the phone with Sarah the next morning as she retold her experience in the room with Jordan, Chris, and little Ellie. I will never forget watching Chris carry a tiny wooden box through the woods to lay his precious baby girl's body to rest and how all a sudden our "young" friends didn't seem so young anymore. I remember telling myself never to forget any of it, and to never again take for granted my motherhood and my three healthy, living children. Never forgetting was, and still is, the best way I knew to honor the memory of Ellie and her beautiful parents.

The days and months after Ellie went to Heaven I remember trying to be intentional. One thing you should all know about Jordan is she is the realest person I know. She has no idea how to "put on airs" or be fake. It is one of my favorite things about her. Between my direct intentionality and her gift of being able to "keep it real," we all found a way to walk together with forward motion through the grief. This is not to say the walk was an easy one. It was raw and hard; but the small, close-knit community that surrounded the Tates during that time did not shy away from the pain. Instead we loved them fiercely and patiently.

Then in February, 8 months after Ellie died, I found out I was pregnant. I knew that Jordan and Chris had talked about having another baby and I also knew that anything and everything which had to do with babies was just plain hard for Jordan. So I prayed a LOT and waited for a "good" time to tell her. I called her and told her the news and she handled it like a champ. We even talked lightly of how cool it would be to be pregnant together. As you know, a few months later that became a reality and we were all overjoyed at this amazing chance to redeem the Tate's parenthood. We only saw each other a few times during the early days of Jordan's pregnancy with Elsie, because they had moved several hours away. We did get a sweet visit in April. It was a short but special time and I remember noting how Jordan already had the "pregnancy glow." Seeing them then and how much hope they were holding for the sweet baby in Jordan's womb just made the news we got a couple of months later that much more horrifying. When we were told that Elsie's condition was nearly the same as her sister's I was in shock. I couldn't believe this was happening again. Then I was just angry, like straight up pissed off! Jordan told us of how her and Chris planned to handle Elsie's pregnancy, with fewer doctor visits and such. This time we also prayed but it was different and if I am honest it was harder. Being pregnant myself I did feel a need to guard my heart some from the profound weight of the grief I felt for my friends. I could have spent my entire third trimester in despair but I knew that was not what God, or Jordan, would want. Our friends and their hearts were never far from our minds though. When we learned our fourth baby was also going to be our fourth son we started praying about what his name would be. Fairly quickly we decided to name him Solace which means "comfort, particularly in a time of grief." One night as I was praying for Jordan I felt God just drop the idea of making Solace Jordan's namesake right into my Spirit. As Jordan mentioned previously, I wanted to honor her motherhood and I loved the idea of my son carrying the name of the bravest person I know.

As you know, Elsie went to be with her sister two days after Christmas. I just remember sitting on the cold ground in my driveway and crying. I cried for the suffering my friends were experiencing but I mostly I just cried for the injustices of it all. Here I was with my fourth healthy baby and my friends were once again going home with empty arms. It felt so unfair and I experienced what I can only describe as a form of survivor's guilt. We packed up the next week to head down to Elsie's service. We spent the morning of the service with the Tates and our other close friends. I had brought Solace with us because he was nursing and Jordan had asked specifically to see him. I had made arrangements for him to stay with my mom during the service because, well… who brings a baby to a baby's funeral? However, as the day went by it became obvious that he was living up to his name and bringing comfort to Jordan. I decided the best thing to do was just ask Jordan what *she* wanted. She said she wanted him there so he stayed. We definitely got some unusual looks from people having him there, but I didn't care. After the service was over Jordan carried Solace around for hours. At one point my husband came up to me to say that we needed to leave to get back to our other kids. I asked him if he was willing to take Solace from Jordan because I was not. We stayed for another hour. I had learned that the best way to love them through their grief was to ask what they needed and then try to give them that. Too often I think we try to give people what *we* think they need instead of just asking. If they don't know what they need, we should be willing to just sit there and be with them.

I never put expectations on Jordan or Chris to act or feel a certain way. If they wanted to be alone, I let them. If they wanted to talk about the girls, I let them. If they cussed and punched the wall, I didn't judge them. If they didn't want to come to a mutual friend's baby shower, I didn't try to talk them into it.

We have also never shied away from referencing the girls or bringing them up in conversation. I know that, at least for Jordan, it means a lot to her that Ellie and Elsie are thought about, and not forgotten. In truth, though they lived here on Earth for only mere minutes their lives have had a profound impact on my world. Although I never knew them or held them, their legacy changed my life. I would liken it to being left a large inheritance by some wealthy relative you have never met. The Tate sisters have given me an ability to embrace the suffering and celebrate the joys of this life with a depth I never knew before.

In Ephesians 3 Paul writes a prayer; he prays that the recipients of his letter would be able to "grasp how wide and long and his and deep the love of Christ is." However, right before that, in verse 17, he lays out that this will be possible because they are "rooted and established in love." Our hearts will gain the richness of this truth when we choose to walk alongside the broken and suffering. When we choose to love others in their grief and take on their burdens as our own, the vastness of God's love is unleashed.

We as a culture have very little tolerance for things that make us uncomfortable or that cause us pain. We would just as soon avoid them at all costs or skim over them like the headlines that pop up on our Facebook feeds. We are just plain bad at walking with the broken and suffering. We want our friends who are going through hard things to just get over it so we can have the old them back. We'd prefer to not deal with their mess. Even in church culture, we are mostly clueless as to what it means to walk with someone through grief. I hope you don't ever have to walk with a loved one through tragedy, but chances are if you are reading this book that is not the case. So I want to recognize the choice you have made to try to love someone well through their darkest days. You have chosen what most would not choose, or maybe simply did not know how to do. Before I met Jordan, I am not sure I knew how either. Like I said, our American culture, as a whole, has become unacquainted with real grief and suffering. What I have offer you is the truth of my experience and the richness it has brought to my heart. Yes, friend, walking with the broken will bring a richness your heart has yet to experience.

20

Our Healthy Baby

When I started writing this book, I had no idea how or when our family would grow. I wanted to continue writing without the pressure to provide a perfect, happy ending to our story about loss. My intent was to convey the message that, even in the absence of the blessing of children, there is hope to be felt and life to be chosen. I hesitated to write about the child that entered our lives because I know that not everyone reading this has gotten to a place where reading about healthy children and life after loss isn't tainted with sorrow and tension. Yet, at the same time, I realized that the life of our son is so perfectly woven into the story of his older sister that I would be remiss not to talk of him.

Two weeks after Elsie passed away, we dove into the process of domestic adoption. There is a verse in Proverbs that described those couple of weeks post-Elsie perfectly. It says, "Hope deferred makes the heart sick, but a longing fulfilled is a tree of life." My heart felt sick. My heart felt so incredibly sick. All I could feel were my empty arms, and I desperately longed for motherhood on this side of life. I knew that the average wait time for domestic adoption was around a year, so I figured we could get licensed and at least have an open door to parenthood. I just needed to know we were moving towards having a little one at home with us. The house felt empty, and the absence of the little voices of my girls and the pitter patter of little feet felt haunting. Our homestudy went without smoothly and within a matter of one month we were considered an "active and waiting" family.

Chris wasn't quite as ready to adopt. We're talking two weeks after Elsie here. I don't blame him. This was most definitely an area in which one of us (he) sacrificed greatly for the other (me). I was desperate. I felt myself constantly slipping into hopelessness, wondering if I would ever hold a child of mine in my arms. Chris saw the ache of my heart and was able to admit that he couldn't fully understand what it was like for me, nor could I for him. When we weighed out all that needed to be considered before moving forward with adoption, the scale only barely tipped into my favor of wanting to adopt immediately. There were a million reasons why we should have waited, and a million and one reasons why we should have moved forward.

I don't think that there is ever a one-size-fits-all for this type of thing. I know there isn't. One would like to think that the solution would be more clear after a situation likes ours, but the truth of the matter is that we are all so incredibly different. If we hadn't chosen to adopt just yet, I know that we would be okay. Starting the licensing process did not make us okay. It didn't magically bring the resolution we craved. Had a baby arrived at our doorstep moments later, we would still have come to the conclusion that a healthy baby will never replace the hurt. We recognized that we were in pain, and we were determined to pay attention to any red flags that would come our way. We committed to being honest with one another if we felt we were trying to force a situation that just was not in our favor.

It didn't take long at all for us to become licensed to adopt. I should add that Chris truly would have waited much longer to begin this whole process, but he also can't deny how perfectly our adoption story played out. We started fundraising immediately and prepared our hearts to wait as the average length of a domestic adoption was twelve months. In the world of domestic adoption, you get presented to a birth family through a short booklet that includes photographs of your family, and a brief history of your life together, and why you desire to adopt. Our booklet included how we met, our hobbies, a description of the town we lived in, the story of Ellie and Elsie, and our heart for adoption.

We were presented to three families before we matched with our son; none of those presentations felt as intense and positively overwhelming as they did when we were presented to the birth mother of our son. We didn't know what it would feel like to match, but the previous presentations just didn't feel quite right. The day we were presented to our son's birth mother, I was on pins and needles. I felt so connected to this little boy who was already born and I had no idea why. I kept feeling as though my heart would break if she did not pick us. I knew that these feelings didn't mean she would pick us. I know that many adoptive families experience these same emotions and then are not chosen. I just hoped and prayed more than I had before that this was it. It absolutely blew my mind that two days earlier we had no idea this little boy existed, and that now we were staring at the clock and our phones anxiously to see if he would become our son. He was born and waiting in Alabama to be matched with a family who could come get him that same week and welcome him into a forever family.

We didn't know it yet, but his birth mother was moved by our book specifically because of the story of our daughters. As we waited anxiously in South Carolina, she told the agency that she felt connected to us, just as I had felt connected to them. She chose us to be her son's parents, and we found out at around eight o'clock that night, just after we had determined that she must have chosen another family. It is the most breathtaking thing of all that the story of our first two children would be the reason we matched with our third. Everything about their story is interwoven beautifully and painfully and profoundly into his.

I got a phone call from our agency, and I fell to my knees and wept. I called everyone I knew to tell them we had a son. It felt so surreal. It felt the way I imagined it would feel to know we were pregnant with a healthy baby. There was this amazing anticipation and pure, unhindered excitement. The best part was that I had continuously gone to the Lord in prayer with my fears about waiting through another mother's pregnancy. In most cases, adoptive parents match with birth mothers who are in their last half of their pregnancy. It is normal for adoptive parents to wonder if the mother will change her mind and decide to parent the child. I knew that, for me, it would be normal to wonder if the baby was truly healthy and free of complications, as worry was all I ever knew of pregnancy.

In His kindness, the Lord matched us with a child

who was already born and whose mother already had her heart set on entrusting him to us, a sacrifice I will never truly understand. His mother spent time with him in the hospital, and the photographs of the two of them together melt my heart. She had nothing but love in her eyes for him, yet she felt as though we could provide a life for him that she couldn't. I know what it feels like to leave the hospital with empty arms. I will forever be incapable of expressing my gratitude towards her.

She wrote us a letter telling us how wonderful it is to be a parent, and how she wanted to give her son to us as a gift. It will be my joy to tell our son, Shepherd, of her selfless heart and of her deep love and commitment to him. Tears fill my eyes as I write this, not able to understand how gracious God was to have this family enter our lives. I am barely able to comprehend the fact that she considered our sweet Ellie and Elsie as she turned the pages of our book. I am barely able to comprehend the fact that she felt as though our losses would drive us to love her son the way she wished for him to be loved. I cannot pretend to know if she would have picked us had Ellie and Elsie not been a part of our story, but I love that Shepherd's sisters are one of the major reasons our arms our now full with a beautiful, bouncy, healthy boy.

We had about a week to prepare to bring our

son home, so we frantically accumulated all of the "necessities" needed to care for a newborn in a hotel room in another state. We didn't keep many baby-related items around the house before matching with him, because seeing them made our hearts ache too deeply. But we did set up Elsie's crib during our pregnancy, and it remained up. The thought of placing Shepherd into her crib for the first time dropped me to my knees.

In case this adoption process wasn't going beautifully enough, the Lord took care of an even more mindblowing detail. Twenty nine years prior to Shepherd's adoption, my parents gave birth to their first baby. I won't go into details about her whole story, because it is not my story to tell, but she passed away as a baby in a car accident before any of my other siblings or I were born. My parents know loss. They know grief. They know all of the complicated mess that is living life without one of your children.

We weren't able to drive to Alabama until he was ten days old. We matched when he was three days old, and then it took us the rest of those days to get all of the paperwork processed. In Alabama, birth parents have five days to change their minds about the adoption, so our agency wanted to protect us emotionally by not allowing us to meet him before that time. We waited, quite impatiently, for the days to pass, and we continued filling out mountains of paperwork in the meantime. We were finally cleared to make the trip on May 8th, 2015.

May 8th is the birthday of my older sister. My parent's first baby. A day that, for so many years, brought the sting of loss and painful memories to the forefront of their minds. It was now the day we would officially bring a healthy baby into our family. These hints of redemption are the business of our Father in Heaven.

Meeting Shepherd was one of the greatest moments of my life.

In a room with my husband, parents, and youngest brother, I couldn't stop crying as I stared at the face of my son. The first time I held him felt as if I had known him for a lifetime. He had already been engraved onto my heart in the most profound way. My life felt like a dream. A couple of days later it was Mother's Day. It was the first Mother's day since Ellie that didn't feel devastating. My heart and my arms were full. All five of us passed him around, all day, every day, holding him and falling in love with him and talking about how perfect he was.

As incredible and surreal as the whole experience was, it also felt so normal. He felt as though he had always belonged to us, and I mean that with the highest respect and utmost love towards the beautiful individuals who created him and the beautiful mother who carried him. He didn't leave any of our arms until we had to put him down to change him or put him in his car seat to travel somewhere. We spent a few more days in Alabama while our paperwork processed, and then we brought our son home. It was incredibly challenging to process his birth mother's loss. I know what it feels like to leave the hospital with empty arms. Even in the light of her choice to place him with us, I know that grief does not discriminate when it comes to a mother's love. I cherish the words from his mother and the photographs of them together. Her face conveys nothing but pride, love, and longing. Because of Ellie and Elsie, it is not lost on me that her greatest loss is my greatest joy. I think of her every day.

Having a child home with us does not erase the longing for our girls, but it certainly soothes our hearts. Ellie and Elsie have given me one of the greatest gifts of all time: I can never take this precious life for granted. Even during the challenging moments as a parent, through the sleepless nights and the days filled with baby tears, it is all a gift. It's all a miracle. I choose his snuggles over dishes and laundry. I stare at his face for hours on end. I thank God every time I hear his cry.

I still fight the triggers that spin me into a place of sorrow, but I have also tasted the goodness of God and the hope of life. I am not entitled to anything on this earth. In fact, what I deserve is far worse than what I have faced. I am not entitled to a perfect adoption story and I do not feel as though these trials somehow earn me healthy children in the future. Yet in the face of this truth, we hold our son who is healthy and happy and perfect. I wholeheartedly believe that, in the end of it all, we will see a day where there will be no more death, no more crying, and no more pain. It is because of Him that I am sustained. It is because of Him that breath fills my lungs. It is because of Him that the sorrow cannot destroy me. No matter what happens to me physically, my soul is anchored with hope, and that doesn't mean I always feel hopeful.

As I finish writing these words, two years have already passed. Two years have passed since my second daughter left this earth. Two years later, I still struggle with each new pregnancy announcement. I know that a life robbed of the joy of my first two children is not an easy life to live. I know that no amount of time can rid me of the memory of feeling the bodies of my sweet girls turn cold right in my arms. Never will I forget kissing their faces. Never will I forget the way they smelled, that sweet newborn baby smell. I know that there will be difficulties unforeseen, as well as seasons of time that don't carry as much of a sting.

What I cannot do is take away the pain and the heartache of loss with any of my words. What I can do, is this: Charge you to be courageous in your moving forward. Courage means getting out of bed when you'd rather stay. It means crying in front of people you trust because it hurts too much that day. It means sharing your story in hopes that others will find comfort. Even if only so that they can rest peacefully in the knowledge that they aren't alone. Press forward and onward and towards all of the life that is ahead. For the pain you have endured will only make the joyous moments sweeter. Courage can look like any number of things. The only thing it doesn't look like is quitting. So don't.

Printed in the United States
By Bookmasters